25⁰⁰

INWARD JOURNEY

Ross Macdonald

EDITED BY

Ralph B. Sipper

1984

Cordelia Editions : Santa Barbara

Contents

INWARD JOURNEY

It is our inward journey that leads us through time—forward or back, seldom in a straight line, most often spiraling.

Eudora Welty
One Writer's Beginnings

THE SCENE OF THE CRIME

Editor's note: "The Scene Of The Crime" was originally read by Ross Macdonald at the University of Michigan in 1954. It was recorded for phonograph use at that time by the University. This text, slightly edited, is a transcription of the recording.

Ross Macdonald

The Scene of the Crime

After writing a mystery novel a year for the last ten years, I would like to take a little time out and survey the field. It isn't easy, I find, for a writer to step back from the work he is hotly engaged in and discuss it rationally and objectively. Everything is strangely out of focus. The perspective alters from moment to moment, which is why I shall probably contradict myself. Mountains appear to be molehills, and vice versa, and one's own little anthill shrinks into appalling insignificance. Which is about the only direct comment I can afford to make on my own work. If I were to discuss it, I'd have to criticize it honestly, and that would be exceedingly painful to everyone, especially to me. The work of earlier and better writers will serve to illustrate my remarks, for the most part.

Though it is one of the dominant literary forms of our age, the mystery has received very little study. Scholars generally reserve it for their leisure hours: when they put on their judicial robes they're inclined to hale it out of critical court. Mystery writers generally have to work too hard applying what they know, to learn the techniques of expressing it in criticism. Or like Graham Greene they refuse to take their mystery writing seriously, though many readers including myself consider Greene's mystery novels his best work. In the absence of a body of criticism on which one might depend, one is reduced to a rather opinionated statement of what seems personally important to oneself. I can only hope that these unsupported opinions will not seem insupportable to other people.

Although I am a kind of popular artist, I have no very clear idea of what a popular art is. I think I know what an art is, but it is easier to know art when you see it than it is to define it. Without attempting a definition of my own, may I simply repeat the commonly accepted idea that a work of art is an expression in words or music or line, an imaginative expression of the artist's interest in and understanding of life, which the imaginations of other people are willing to accept and able to enjoy. This life which the artist imitates, if I may use the world of Aristotle and Coleridge, is the sum-total of human experience or any aspect of it which arouses the imagination's interest. This isn't to say with some Neo-Aristotelians that the artist takes the form of his work directly form external life. The form of a work seems to be derived partly form the shape of the artist's thought and temperament, so that it becomes the vehicle of his personal intention in writing or composing; partly and often predominantly from observed life; and always, too, from the tradition or convention which the artist chooses to support him in his purposes. Popular art so-called can often be distinguished from unpopular or highbrow art by the artist's choice of convention. Thus a writer who works in a recognized popular form like the mystery novel is ipso facto considered a popular artist, his novels popular art. Probably this matter of choice of convention is the most commonly accepted differentia of popular art.

Other differentiae are the size of the audience for which the artist works, or at which he aims; the quality of the audience; the quality of the work itself; the simplicity and clarity of its communication, which depends in turn on a widely shared community of interest between artist and audience. It seems to be generally assumed among intellectual people, if their opinions are honestly represented by the little magazines, that the presence of this widely shared community of feeling in a work of popular art deprives it of any high value or function, in a word that popular art is inferior art, an idiot sinister offspring of the muses. And there is plenty of evidence to support this opinion.

Most slick magazine fiction, for example, is pretty bad, often indistinguishable in content and meaning and intention from the advertising that frames it, or which it frames. From the words and music that assail our ears on radio and television, we often turn with relief to the singing commercials. But the question worth asking is whether the vast and empty and mechanical output of the big slicks and the record factories is really popular art. This false art, if I may beg the question I have raised, rushes into the vacuum where the real thing should be flourishing, or smothers it before it has a chance to develop or be seen. I call it false because it is composed on a dishonest basis, because the community of thought and feeling on which it purports to found itself no longer exists, or never did exist. Remember that the man in the street for whom it is supposed to be produced is almost certainly a high school graduate. He doesn't believe that virtue is financially rewarded, or even that it should be; that women are composed in equal parts of Joan of Arc and rosewater and Marilyn Monroe; that love is something Platonic yet titillating which ends with marriage; that children are wiser than their elders; that a man is either a hero or a coward; or that the great stakes of life are sexual and monetary exclusively. The daydream art based on these false assumptions may serve to fill his empty time but it can't fill his imagination. It fills the old bottles with carbonated water, instead of wine. The consequences are that popular music has literally fallen into the hands of adolescent children. The work of a good popular composer like Ellington is seldom heard in the land, except over the high-fidelity systems. The big magazines whose factual material is so often interesting seem to edit their fiction for victims of adult-infantism or frustrated addicts of mechanical wish-fulfillment. And as our false popular art turns away from life, the man in the street turns away from it, and is in danger of being left, as Wyndham Lewis prophesied, without any art at all, without any real assistance in coordinating the deep and flashing insights into the human condition which every normal man experiences and which true popular art has always embodied.

It would be wrong, I think, to blame the man in the street for this situation, or to blame the editors and publishers and producers. The crime of irresponsibility is a general one. We are all victims, willing or unwilling, of a civilization in which minds and their products are bought and sold. I don't mean that we have to succumb to economic and social determinism. The fabric of a society is still woven of little individual acts of will and strands of intention. Our individual acts of will and threads of thought can change the overall pattern in the long run, especially when they are the thoughts and acts of intellectuals and artists. Since I have a foothold, a rather uneasy foothold, in both camps I can appropriately lay the blame for our present cultural impasse at the feet of intellectuals and artists. We are the ones, in the long run, who determine the shape of society, the originators of the thought which informs the leviathan with life and purpose. But we unacknowledged legislators seem to be losing our grip on the forces we used to handle and control. Often we seem to sit as a sort of rump parliament debating the issues of past revolutions in politics or art or sensibility or ethics, while an actual revolution is going on just around the corner, without the benefit of our intervention. And the man in the street, who looks to us for leadership, for community of interest and of purpose, the man in the street hears only a murmur of voices speaking a language he doesn't quite understand, though he would like to.

The picture I have sketched is in poster colors, and exaggerated for propaganda purposes. Qualification is needed. Out of each half-dozen men in the street, one has attended college. Hemingway's last book, a fine piece of primitive if not of popular art, reached several million readers. Mass publication of books, mass reproduction of music and pictures, broadcast good things along with the chaff more widely than ever before. Still much of the wheat falls on barren ground, and some of it is poisoned. Certain writers of the cloaca-and-dagger school represent to my mind the ultimate degradation of popular art. I hope that it is ultimate. And the gulf between high culture and low culture which partisan intellectuals deplore is indubitably and existentially there. It causes isolation and frustration on the one hand, emptiness and shallowness on the other. Our high culture is preoccupied with the infinite subtleties of psychology and morals, of abstract values in general; our low culture with things, with animal satisfactions still masquerading in Victorian moonlight. While I don't claim that art alone can cure an advanced schizophrenia, I do think aesthetic therapy is preferable to atomic shock treatment, and should certainly accompany it.

I suppose that *Huckleberry Finn* did as much as any other single human art, to put the divided country back together again, in a different shape. Huck's voyage was successful, as we are gradually learning, because he took Jim along with him. And it is interesting that our finest novel, perhaps our one American epic, should also be our most popular novel. Popular in every sense, Mark Twain's book speaks to the people in their own tongue, reaches them with the intimacy of their heartbeat. It is popular art *in excelsis,* pawky and racy and colloquial and funny, just as the *Odyssey* probably was to a Greek. Yet it has the quiet depth and grandeur of a classic, and we can read it once a year and not come to the end of its meanings. It is both popular and the highest art. And with the finest works of other countries, the plays of Shakespeare and Ibsen, the novels of Dickens and Dostoevsky, the *Odyssey* and the Saga of Grettir the Strong, it suggests that the greatest artists draw their strength from the popular earth like the legendary giant, and return their strength to its source.

Mark Twain was just about the last great American novelist who wrote to a whole civilization, considered both horizontally and vertically, as Dickens, or perhaps Kipling, was the last English one. Kipling's disciples Crane and London, Zola's disciple Norris, tried to carry on the tradition of writing for everyone. Crane died young, unsustained by his culture and burnt out. London never learned to develop his talent, and ended hacking for magazines. Norris made a valiant attempt to project a democratic novel of the future. Though his theory was rather crudely quantitative and over-optimistic, his practice very uneven, disrupted by native romanticisms and undigested importations from Europe, I think that Norris is a figure worth looking back to. In his time our culture was already tearing at the seams. If Norris's style and vision failed to pull it together, he saw the problem and did what he could to solve it. Since Norris, the isolation of the serious American novelist, which had already begun with Melville and Henry James, and the splitting off of the intellectual from his environment, have proceeded *pari passu* and apace. If the life which Norris saw around him through his rather imperfect naturalistic spectacles was raw and crude, he had at least the courage to embrace it. He wrestled leviathan to a draw, let us say, and even taught it a couple of new holds. But the prototype of the modern American intellectual, at least in the literary field, is less like Norris than like Emily Dickinson. A superior artist, perhaps, but useless, because she was unread by a generation which was starved for poetry.

I don't mean to express anti-intellectual sentiments. Intellectuals and their unidentical twins, creative artists, are indispensable, and their gradual withdrawal from the modern life of the western world is tragic. Doubly tragic, because it is also a withdrawal of life from the artists and intellectuals. Their expatriation, either actual or psychic, helps to account for the number of one-book and two-book men in our modern literary history. The imaginative aloofness verging on contempt which so many of our good writers have shown towards American life, their embarrassment in the presence of their own background and tradition, has not only tended to deprive us of a popular literature, but has hamstrung the writers themselves in mid-course of their careers. A Hemingway, who might have written our yet unwritten great depression novel, gave us instead *To have and Have Not* and *Green Hills of Africa,* works of botched and wasted genius. Even our lovely Fitzgerald, whose *Gatsby* is a heartbreaking fable of the artist's alienation from his society, even Fitzgerald wandered in pursuit of false gods and bright Medusas, and took his talent along with him. When Dick Diver returned from Europe and settled down as a general practitioner in upstate New York, his story ended: "his latest note was postmarked from Hornell, New York, which is some distance from Geneva and a very small town; in any case he is almost certainly in that section of the country, in one town or another." Fitzgerald no longer cares what happens to Diver. He is back in America. He has dropped out of the international set. His life is finished, but it is hard to see why. Another novelist, a Faulkner for example, might have begun another and greater novel precisely where Fitzgerald ended *Tender Is the Night.* There is a sense in which Faulkner did just that, in *Soldier's Pay,* the first of his tremendous cycle. It is significant that the most prolific imagination of our time and place has nourished itself by cultivating its own local wilderness. And it falls very pat with my theme that William Faulkner is, among other things, a mystery novelist.

I wrote in an introduction to one of Faulkner's stories in 1946: "Though he helped to write the screen play for *The Big Sleep,* William Faulkner is not usually thought of when mystery authors are mentioned. The fact is that he had made a more original and imaginative contribution to the mystery form than anyone since Poe. . . . His strange and wonderful novel, *Sanctuary,* shrugged off by its author as a pot-boiling thriller "deliberately conceived to make money," has been claimed for literature by critics here and abroad. Andre Malraux has described it as "the detective story usurping tragedy." The mystery technique which Faulkner has applied to the manipulation of difficult material, and developed to such a pitch of grace and subtlety, can be traced in some of his other novels, *Absalom, Absalom!* for example, and in many of his short stories. "A Rose for Emily," his most frequently reprinted story is a beautifully worked out mystery solved in a final sentence which no one who has read it will ever forget.

Since 1946, Faulkner has confirmed the suggestion that the

mystery tradition is one of the sources of his art, by publishing a volume of detective stories, *Knight's Gambit,* and a novel, *Intruder in the Dust,* which is probably our most ambitious American mystery novel.

I don't mean to try to borrow Faulkner's authority in support of any such theses as these: that the mystery form is the gateway to literary grace, or that we mystery writers are budding Faulkners, or that Faulkner's greatness is dependent on his use of this popular literary convention. Still the fact remains that he did use it, that the narrative techniques of the popular mystery are closely woven into the texture of much of his work, and that the books in which they are most evident were the only ones of his to reach a large audience in this country. His example certainly proves that the mystery tradition is available for the purposes of the highest art. Without suggesting that it is capable of producing or sustaining more than one Faulkner, I do believe it is a form which has much to offer writers who are interested in close and serious communication and a popular audience. I think I can say why it first attracted me. I was eager to make a living by my pen, no easy job in these or any times. Yet I wasn't willing to become a mere dream-manufacturer or entertainer. I wanted to write as well as I possibly could, to deal with life-and-death problems in contemporary society. And the form of Wilkie Collins and Graham Greene, of Hammett and Chandler, seemed to offer me all the rope I would ever need. The potentialities of the detective story are still largely unrealized. Some of its potentialities may be indicated by turning back to Poe and trying to discover some of the purposes for which he invented it, then looking at what some later writers have done.

While I cannot speak of these historical matters with the precision of a literary scholar, I hope that those who *are* literary scholars will allow me a little prosaic license in sketching what I take to be Poe's historical situation and intention. Like his quondam master Coleridge, Poe stands as an archetype and symbol of the modern isolated literary artist. I suppose *The Ancient Mariner* is the psychological epic of modern man cut off from tradition by the final crumbling of the medieval synthesis, estranged from his fellow men by superior sensibility and insight, and by the commensurate guilt which is the price the poet paid for his insight into the sources of evil in himself. Poe wrote his own prose version of *The Ancient Mariner,* in the remarkable *Narrative of Arthur Gordon Pym,* and made his own grave pilgrimage through the dark night of the soul to the caves of ice. Poe was isolated in his generation by his uniquely deep and sharply felt experience of death, of guilt, of the psychological horror with which a threatened loss of religion haunted him and Coleridge and most of the best minds of the century. And in the midst of a barren culture, a hostile society—the record of Poe's life underlines those adjectives—he was more terribly isolated than any Englishman of his time could be. Yet he was faced by his pioneer genius with the task which Carlos Williams has described in *In the American Grain:* the task of forging means to express his sensibility, to objectify and artistically ameliorate the sense of guilt and horror which he perceived in himself and suffered, perhaps in poetic anticipation, for his society. I am unable to explain, either psychologically or theologically, why Poe was forced to write of death and loss, sin and crime, the dissolution of minds and houses and cities, and of constant and inescapable guilt. No doubt the pains he felt were partly the birth-pangs of a new civilization, the press of a ponderous freedom, the breathless responsibility of an emancipated introspection which was beginning to thread the mammoth caves of the unconscious mind. The new freedom which the nineteenth century found for itself, and for us, was a freedom to know evil as well as good, and Poe was our first completely aware nineteenth century man. I like to think of him as a smaller, intenser, less cultivated Coleridge transported after all to the banks of the Susquehanna. And there is a sense, if I may fetch the fancy a little further, in which Poe's work is the completion of *Christabel.* My fellow admirers of Coleridge will perhaps forgive me for suggesting that *Christabel* is an unfinished mystery novel in verse, whose subject is the elucidation of guilt and its ritual exorcism—a guilt which arises from man's ability to sin against himself, both consciously and unconsciously.

Certainly this is Poe's subject. Let me read a few lines from one of his stories. The lines seem to me to possess a tragic paradoxical insight equal to Kierkegaard's or Dostoevsky's; they and the story express, in fact, the theme of *Crime and Punishment,* without the Russian master's final hope.

> And then came, as if to my final and irrevocable overthrow, the spirit of Perverseness. . . . It was this unfathomable longing of the soul to *vex itself*—to offer violence to its own nature—to do wrong for the wrong's sake only—that urged me to continue and finally to consummate the injury I had inflicted upon

> the unoffending brute. [The brute is The Black Cat, Poe's personal albatross.] One morning, in cool blood, I slipped a noose about its neck and hung it to the limb of a tree—hung it with the tears streaming from my eyes, and with the bitterest remorse of my heart—hung it *because* I knew that it had loved me, and *because* I felt it had given me no reason of offence;—hung it *because* I knew that in so doing I was committing a sin—a deadly sin. . . .

These are the words of an American Raskolnikov expressing the will to evil which modern man accepted as part of the bargain when he took command of his own will. They suggest the satanic pride which was the other side of Rousseau's optimistic coin, the diabolism which Poe's French followers developed to fill the vacuum of their faith, above all the terrible guilt inherent in the freedom to be evil. The scene of the crime for Poe is his own tell-tale heart. I believe that the human propensity for evil, with the concomitant guilt and fear which he felt, is felt by all modern men in varying degrees. Poe used and developed the Gothic tale to a new level, and invented the detective story in order to grasp and objectify the nature of the evil, and somehow place the guilt. That is probably the function of all good detective stories, to confront us imaginatively with evil, to explain it in the course of a narrative which convinces us of its reality, if possible to purge the evil. They reduce to intelligible form the vague shapes of sin and terror and death which haunt us all, and reassure our minds of the power of human virtue, human reason, over human evil. We yield ourselves to an unreal terror in order to have our terror explained away. Yet paradoxically, the very best detective stories present a true vision of evil to which there is no rational counterstatement, and leave a residue of terror and understanding pity, like tragedy itself, which can't be explained away. I am thinking of books like *Sanctuary*, Hammett's *Glass Key*, Chandler's *Farewell My Lovely*, H. C. Branson's remarkable *The Leaden Bubble*, and *Vanish in an Instant*, written by a former Ann-Arborite who shall be nameless.

Returning to Poe, we find in his first detective story, *The Murders in the Rue Morgue*, a strong element of the reassurance I have mentioned, combined with an unflinching attention to the details of atrocity. I don't fully understand the preoccupation with atrocity—one might almost use the word fascination—which characterizes detective stories including my own, and so much other modern fiction.

One of its sources is surely the spiritual malaise, the hypersensitivity to guilt and suffering which I have referred to. But like most psychic facts, it has wide cultural and social bearings. The nineteenth century made the discovery, and bequeathed it to us, that man is indeed a little lower than the angels, and possibly not much higher than the beasts. Such first-rate and tormented geniuses as Poe and Dostoevsky and Dickens witnessed in the laboratories of their imaginations the human consequences of scientific and philosophic half-truth; and foresaw the terrible process of osmosis by which these consequences have emerged into actuality in our era of activity. Of course Dostoevsky and Dickens, no more than Hemingway or Faulkner, did not have to depend on their imaginations to know physical consequences of evil. Neither did Poe, with wide and agonized experience of pre-Civil War America. There are other reasons for the extraordinary interest which modern writers (and readers) have displayed in criminals and their doings. The Byronic artist from Byron himself to Hemingway, his offspring the Bohemian artist—one thinks of Wilde in Reading Gaol or Proust in the last stages of his life-novel—these men for more than personal reasons have been at odds with their society. Outlaws of thought and convention, in varying degrees, they found it easy to assimilate themselves to the genuine outlaw elements of society.

One can go further and suggest that many modern writers have felt the need to undergo and imaginatively express the sharpest pains and bitterest moral dilemmas of our society. In a period of fear and loss, the artist deliberately assumes the experiences of the fearful and the lost—voluntarily submits himself to the involuntary anguish of the criminal, the insane, the dispossessed. Such submission is motivated by something more than masochistic impulse to self-abasement, though these motives may play a part in it. It arises from a need, which every artist feels in some degree, to assume responsibility for his civilization, to know and realize the implications of his society. This act of shamanization, to borrow Wyndham Lewis's anthropological metaphor, this act by which the artist becomes the frockless or renegade priest or scapegoat of his community, can be performed even by secondary writers, in which category most mystery writers fall. Lewis's own novel, *The Vulgar Streak,* which incidentally has a mystery structure, provides an example illustrating his critical theory. The hunting down of a confidence man, who is undoubtedly one of the author's *personae,* becomes a fable of the guilt of an unreal and collapsing society.

Nelson Algren's *Man with the Golden Arm,* also a novel of crime and detection and suicide, is the fine work of an American *shaman.* Devoid of easy hope as such work is, it is an ethical work to say, "You live badly, my friends," to demonstrate how and why. It casts light and compassion in the dark places where it is very badly needed.

The writer who is forced by inner and outer pressures to deal with crime and its consequences cannot, if he is to perform any function of conciliation and redemption, simply wallow in brute fact. Atrocity must be immobilized in some way, if not neutralized, taken up into an intelligible pattern and subordinated to something more human than itself. If the purpose of old tragedy was to subordinate the evil and horrible to an inhuman fate, the purpose of Poe's detective story is to subordinate it to human reason. By a strange paradox, which may contain significance for us, the tale of the bloody murders in the Rue Morgue is a very hymn to analytic reason, intended, as Poe wrote later, "to depict some very remarkable features in the mental character of my friend, the Chevalier C. Auguste Dupin." Poe himself called his detective stories "tales of ratiocination." The first and most interesting of them, (though *The Purloined Letter* has greater technical virtue) *Rue Morgue* sets itself the problem of rationalizing the occurrence of a seemingly impossible horror. I use the word rationalize in two senses. In the first place, the story explains, with a show of logic which is just a little preposterous and pretentious—not unlike the logic of Sherlock Holmes—a strange double killing whose details are too well known to be rehearsed by me. Dupin's inexorable process of elimination provides us, to use one of Poe's favorite words, with a "rationale" of horror. Dupin's "frigid and abstract" reason—Poe's adjectives—is made to triumph by remote control over an antagonist which is described as follows: "Gnashing its teeth, and flashing fire from its eyes, it flew upon the body of the girl and embedded its fearful talons in her throat, retaining its grasp until she expired." I have suggested that this is rationalization in a second sense. Since Poe has long since been claimed for symbolism by the French, I may be excused for looking for symbolic meaning in one of his best-known stories. It presents us near the beginning with a scene of "horrible mystery." The wrecked apartment behind the locked door, with the corpse of a woman thrust up the chimney, seems to me to show the earmarks of a dream symbol, a nightmare symbol, and Dupin's ratiocination about it bears a curious resemblance to the elucidation of a bad dream. Superficially considered, the explanation is clever, and was once, I know, surprising. But as an explanation of human guilt, which the reader is led to expect by the terrible images invoked, it turns out to be evasive and disappointing. Evasive, that is, unless we recognize a symbolic intention which elevates the ape into a human symbol, a symbol of a perhaps unconscious guilt. I suggest that the story's intention is to represent and then to purge such guilt, that Dupin stands for the human reason in conflict with the nightmare forces of the mind, and ultimately mastering them. The reader shares the conflict and the final mastery, though he is preserved by technical barriers from a too immediate participation in it. He sees the hairy ape, the Gorgon locks, at second and third hand. Reassured by Dupin's calm couchside manner, he leaves the story, all but persuaded that the ape is safe in his cage, and that he really meant no harm in the first place. Detective stories frighten the reader in order to reassure him. The best of them leave a residue of horror. But he has gained some knowledge of the ape and of himself. Poe protests too much that there is nothing human in its voice. The scene of the crime persists in the imagination, and we recall the author's fascination with the death of women.

I suggest that Dupin's analysis is a false analysis which permits both author's and readers' imaginations to endure the dream. Or should I say that protagonist and antagonist stand for opposite poles of the human mind, that the story brings them together in conflict and restores them to a proper relationship. The ape's qualities of violence and concupiscence, anger and fear, are subordinated to the more human reason. The scene of the crime is still the human heart.

The technical structure which leads by slow and logical stages to, or near to, the roaring center of the maze is characteristic of the detective story. The detective Dupin, the kind of Virgil or rather a dehydrated Byron who leads a first-person narrator through a kind of hell—this detective is also typical. There must be a reason deeper than the obvious technical advantages for ths splitting of the protagonist into two parts (and perhaps the criminal ape is still a third part) since so many of Poe's followers from Gaboriau through Doyle to Rex Stout have imitated it. Of course it helps to postpone the solution, and at the same time to eliminate the inessential. It enables the author to present his hero, who is so often a projection of himself, without embarrassment and without blushing. It assists the author in dealing with dangerous emotional material, while preserving his literary *sangfroid.* Compare the cool astringent tone of any of the Dupin stories, with the hysteria and melodrama of some of those where the "hero" speaks for himself. "The Black Cat" for instance.

Yet all of these explanations seem to miss the main point, the root of the author's intention. This detective Dupin, this Holmes, even this Nero Wolfe, in spite of Watson's tongue-cluckings and Archie's irony, is offered as an authentic hero to be respected and admired by the reader. One projection of the author, the narrator, is made to assume a posture of more or less blind ambition before another persona of the author, the detective hero. The reader is invited to share this posture, to place his eager little Watsonian hand in Holmes's, let us say, and stroll through hell. A literally split man becomes a sort of superman accompanied by an adoring disciple. Such a pattern becomes very clear in the Holmes stories, but its origin in the Dupin stories is almost equally evident. It is hardly too much to say that Holmes is a caricature of the original, Dupin-cum-laudanum. Both, I should say, are wish-fulfillment figures, projections of the nineteenth-century artist that succeed by an esoteric and superior craft in mastering the problems of an alien and dangerous environment. Dupin is a declassed aristocrat, as Poe's heroes tend to be, a projection of the artist who has lost the sense of place because he has lost has foothold in tradition. He lives a nocturnal and bookish life like a Huysmann hero. He has no social life, only one friend. What sets him apart from others is his superiority. His willingness to think and act cuts him off from other men, and even from his more comfortable self. He sees through men with the X-ray eyes of a preternaturally developed reason—a faculty which Poe himself possessed in the highest degree. It is hard not to see in Dupin a compensation for Poe's lack of recognition as an intellectual leader in his society. Recalling Poe's dream of an intellectual hierarchy governing the mental life of the nation, himself at its head, one is tempted to interpret these stories, under one aspect, as an attempt at compensation. Dupin's outwitting of an unscrupulous politician in *The Purloined Letter,* his solution of an actual New York case in *Marie Roget,* his repeated trumping of the cards held by the Prefect of Police, are Poe's vicarious demonstration of superiority to an indifferent society and its officials. The narrator's admiration for Dupin has elements of self-admiration.

This is harmless enough in Poe's stories, I suppose, but there are disturbing possibilities in the pattern. I will try to illustrate what I mean—if Baker Street Irregulars will lay their pistols down—from the saga of Dupin's most famous avatar, Sherlock Holmes. Not only the character of Sherlock Holmes, but the technique by which he is presented, is based on Poe's technique. The subordination of the narrator to the hero, and through him the subordination of the reader, are taken over from Poe. But the rather hothouse atmosphere of uncritical admiration which is made to surround the hero is brought to boiling point in Dr. Watson's prose. There are also changes in the object of the praise. Dupin, who seems to be primarily a psychologist and literary scholar, though he also moves familiarly in high political circles, has given place to a more modern type. Sherlock Holmes's field of expertness is science, especially chemistry and anatomy. Where Dupin specialized in psychological and linguistic analysis, the more modern Holmes employs the methods of the physical scientist. He is a curious combination of the Bohemian rebel of the Lionel Johnson period—the only woman he really admired was a courtesan—and a modern laboratory criminologist. All of which scarcely makes him a complete man. In fact, a psychiatrist might diagnose his case in terms of manic-depressive and schizoid tendencies. Yet this remarkable creature is presented to us as a master of life. The stories offer repeated demonstrations of the detective's superiority to Dr. Watson, to Lastrade, to everyone else in London and in England. And Watson loves it, if Lastrade does not.

I submit that there is something undignified or worse in the posture of admiration enforced by the Holmes saga towards its hero. The habit of respecting a lone-wolf superman who operates outside and above the law can be dangerous to the health of the imagination. This may seem a humorless and carping criticism. It is true that much of the saga is comic, often intentionally so, and that its author never expected it to be taken too seriously. Yet I think it deserves to be taken seriously. Holmes is the most famous character in modern English fiction. Hundreds of novelists have tried to recreate him in various guises. But Holmes's importance is more than literary. He is the hero of scientism, as his creator intended him to be—perhaps our most significant culture-hero. He is the scientific superman who bids us sit with bated breath while he solves the mysteries of life with his microscope, and denatures death itself with the contents of his test-tubes. He is the investigator who roots out whatever is rotten in the state, the law above the law who asks for no reward except for free indulgence of his vices (this is explicit at the end of *The Sign of the Four*). Nobody asks: who is going to investigate the investigator? and nobody criticizes him. Watson's occasional critical comments are mere conventional sops to the reader. Holmes is above criticism. He is a dedicated man whose life is selfless and wholly employed in regulating other people's lives. If he is not a naked embodiment of the will to power, he certainly represents a blandly inhuman curiosity which resists emotional involvement with any living creature yet seeks in the name of an undiscussed personal vocation to interfere in the activities of others. Only *he* is fitted by training and desire to solve the conundrums of the modern metropolis. And all we ever know is what he chooses to tell us.

It would be ridiculous for anyone to suggest that a fine old pukka sahib like Conan Doyle was in any way capable of intending or perpetrating a threat to free institutions—he was a just and compassionate man, as his live ghost Dickson Carr has shown—or that Holmes was a prototype of the dictatorial mind. Holmes was an expression of a tendency rather than a cause, the literary embodiment of a habit of mind for which literature is not responsible. I mean the habit of deferring to the specialist, of bowing down before the superior wisdom of the dedicated investigator who hates evil more than anyone. His giant lone-wolf figure seems to me to loom yet behind the activities of other investigators whose access to special materials or inner light renders them superior to justice or common sense. I refer of course to the Himmlers and Berias. And I would like to know more of Holmes's motives and private life.

It would be interesting now, if I had time and you had infinite patience, to enter at considerable length into the nineteenth century's achievement in the mystery novel. It reached its peak very early—Reynolds once pointed out, with reference to Michelangelo, that new arts spring full-armed from the head of their first great genius, and leap at once to the height—in *The Brothers Karamazov.* It would be possible to demonstrate that Dostoevsky's masterpiece is a formal psychological mystery novel, complete with unsolved murder, suspects, red herrings, trial of the wrong man, and final solution revealing the least-likely culprit. But it would be out of place to try to claim the greatest of Russian novels for my craft. Let it stand as an example of what in the hands of a master the mystery novel may at any time become: a profound work of philosophic art which gathers into itself the highest and deepest and most dreadful forces of its century. Even a novel like Wilkie Collins's *Woman in White,* though it fades like a shape of fog in the dark sun of Dostoevsky, is more than the progenitor of our modern Daphne du Mauriers, more than a soundly written and brilliantly plotted novel of sensation. It deserves a place in the history of the English novel if the novel is, as Mark Twain said it was, essentially a history of private life, a record of how people live. From the oppression endured by Collins's women, one gets a vivider sense of some of the social aspects of Victorianism than from three volumes of Esme-Wingfield-Stratford. Henry James probably learned from Collins—the dim gray Collins atmosphere and the sad lake of the *Woman in White* recur like a nightmare in *The Turn of the Screw*—and Dickens certainly learned from him.

The Dickens-Collins influence runs two ways, as Dickens's definitive biographer, Edgar Johnson has lately shown. The Collins atmosphere of tattletale gray is the light and dark of the Dickens world filtered through a smaller, more modern mind, less tormented and less hopeful than Dickens was in his last years. Dickens had little or nothing to learn from his protege—Collins except in the matter of plotting; but the novel of sensation exerted a great attraction on his imagination. Plot had always been Dickens's weakness—we recall Poe's deadly foreknowledge of the plot of one of his novels (*Martin Chizzlewit?*)—as it was Collins's strength. Moving in his grim last years towards a sterner unity of intention, Dickens took full advantage of the lesson. It is clear in books like *Great Expectations* and *Our Mutual Friend* that Dickens was ever more intensely urged to probe the darker corners of English life. The novel of sensation and mystery became his chosen instrument, beginning with *Our Mutual Friend.*

Dickens learned from Collins, and demonstrates to us, how wide the dragnet of the mystery form can be flung. Like the picaresque novel of previous centuries, it has vast social range and mobility. A criminal mystery brings together, in fiction and in truth, representatives of every social class and moral category. It places these characters in situations of tension where every word and gesture become, or can be made to seem, revealing. It gives the novelist an opportunity and excuse to return and return again to the problem of evil that obsesses him. It lends itself to the juxtaposition and conflict of classes which are one of the social novelist's main interests, and to the sudden reversals and revelations which Aristotle recommended in tragedy. It is no wonder that Dickens found it useful.

But the traditional mystery form has one great defect as an instrument for fulfilling the intention of a social novelist, or a novelist of character. This is not the ineluctable fact that its subject is crime and death, guilt and punishment. These are the subjects of most tragedy and much serious fiction. I admit that most mysteries including mine are rather too rigidly conventional in structure, but this is the fault of the authors, not the form. A writer like the late Josephine Tey, in *The Franchise Affair*, has shown us how to build an original structure around the crime, or the misdemeanor, of lying. The evil-doers of Faulkner's *Sanctuary* are gunmen, but murder is not the central crime of the book. Its central crime is the destruction of innocence, the symbolic defloration of a great tradition by the rapacious forces of the machine age.

The defect may be stated in this way: the central character is a detective of one kind or another. As I tried to suggest in connection with Sherlock Holmes, a detective or investigator is an incomplete hero in most cases, an inadequate focus for the reader's imaginative interest, a somewhat hypocritical projection for the author's. Detection or investigation is a somewhat ignoble profession for a first-rate hero. It is too unilateral, too ethical. It does not involve enough of the self, and can become an excuse for callousness and cynicism, for shallowness and deliberate non-involvement, for turning away from life towards abstraction. It can, in a word, confirm us in the very failings which it is the novelist's purpose to expunge. The protagonist of any fiction which aims at truth, especially fiction that deals with private and public wrong, should not be too righteous, let alone self-righteous. A hero should be flawed—all the great heroes are—he should be passionately, even guiltily, involved in life on the fulcrum of the scales of justice instead of its custodian. Yet the detective is by definition the representative of law and order and convention. Even Sherlock Holmes, for all his peculiarities, remains a slightly damaged man. And nothing ever happens to him morally, except his passing glance at Irene Adler.

I believe Conan Doyle did make Watson suggest that Holmes could have become the master criminal of his age. Hornung noted the suggestion, and created Raffles, if Raffles can be described as a creation: certainly Raffles has no moral life; he is Hornung's unique contribution to fiction, a one-dimensional character. The one character in every mystery novel who does not have a moral life and is deeply involved with the central crime is the murderer. It is the murderer rather than the detective who must be the center of attention if the mystery is to have a genuine tragic interest. Or at least protagonist and antagonist must come into close and revealing conflict. Revelation is the aim of art, self-knowledge its end. Yet in every formal mystery, right up to the end, the murderer is a sealed book to us. The author does not enter without inhibition into this character's thoughts, or let him voice them. In some ways, then, the form requires an evasion of its professed subject, a means, as I suggested earlier, of leading the reader's mind around the roaring heart of the maze, or showing him as Medusa in a distorting mirror. The element of reassurance which we noted in Poe, becomes a central flaw in the form itself. At its lightest the mystery novel declines into an exercise in shadow-boxing and deserves the pejorative name whodunit. It is a pleasure to play drop-the-handkerchief with Mrs. Christie, or who's-got-the-button with Mr. Gardner, but it doesn't bring us into contact with life. On the contrary. Mr. W. H. Auden has argued from his favored position behind the Kierkegaardian categories that this is what the mystery is for. It transports us, he says, to an Arcadian never-never land where we can take a sedative and relax from the strenuosities of morals. Charles Lamb held a similar view of Congreve's and Wycherley's comedy, but I doubt that Congreve and Wycherley held that view. They were engaged with life, and so are a good many mystery novelists.

To me the real interest and potentiality of the mystery resides in its use for symbolic and psychological and social purposes by writers like Poe and Collins and Dickens. The latter's closest approach to writing a formal mystery novel was, of course, *The Mystery of Edwin Drood.* This grim and atmospheric novel, for all its virtues, provides an example of the defect I have pointed out in the form. Its main figure is the Byronic and Svengali-like music master, John Jasper. His actions and motives are the center of interest throughout. He is the villain-as-hero, a creation worthy of a Webster or Tourneur, and he demands to be treated in terms of tragic insight. But he is not. His actions remain obscure, so very obscure that no one knows for certain how the story should end. The anguished interplay of moral forces that must be going on behind Jasper's iron countenance remains unknown to us. The question why a cathedral choirmaster should murder his nephew, if he did—and that is a question worthy of the very greatest novelist—will remain forever unanswered. Even if Dickens had lived to finish his book, the evasive pattern of the form he chose would have prevented him from writing fully and to the top of his bent about his central character and his central problem. We'd know Jasper only externally until the end, and by that time it would be a little too late. The novel at its best judges and interprets its characters and their development page by page. Some insight is deferred, of course, by every narrative form, to knit the work at the end into a meaningful and gestaltic whole. But the mystery novel defers too much to the end. It forces or permits the novelist to write most of his book, free of any responsibility of being constantly meaningful. And in many cases, *Drood* for one, it forces or permits the novelist to evade full treatment of his professed subject, to prevent human actions of the deepest significance without motivating them adequately or judging them strictly, to invent characters without developing them. It may be that these very limitations recommended the form to Dickens in his tired and premature old age. Obviously he was committed to a final effort to probe the guilts, social and personal, which had long obsessed and tormented him. Jasper is the guilty artist in love with a young girl, a sweet singer whose music is turned cacophonous in his ears. I think he is a persona of the novelist, and that Dickens intended to use him to look deeper into himself than he had ever ventured to look before. He was willing to face Medusa, his will to truth urged him to it, but he lacked the strength for the last tragic effort. The distorting mirror of the mystery form enabled him to present as much as he dared to of his subject: man's will to evil, specifically an artist's destruction of his younger, better self, but he evaded its tragic implications. Generalizing on perhaps inadequate grounds, one might say that the mystery form forces and permits the novelist to write of tragic subjects without facing the responsibilities and implications of tragedy. It may be that we, writers and readers, are unable or unwilling to look directly at tragic reality. It may be that the mystery is a rather inferior substitute for tragedy. It interposes complexity and obstruction between the thought and the deed, the stimulus and the response. It doles out tragedy bit by bit and masks its meaning with all the arts of mystification. It tends to dichotomize life, to divide the sheep from the goats, yet to reserve judgment on which are sheep and which are goats. It sustains a false skepticism which is brought finally to an equally false certainty. Its abstract structure is a cage in which to catch the hairy ape of evil, for the protection and reassurance of the populace. It may be that it is the most popular literary form of a schizophrenic society which does not really know what its left lobe is doing but would like to pretend to itself that it does.

One of the reasons why some of us favor the so-called hardboiled mystery is that it does not hold the problem of evil at arm's length. Now I don't speak for the current truants from the school, the semiliterate hairy apes and the kindergarten Krafft-Ebings. The less said of them the better. And after all, bad prose is essentially a crime against oneself. I speak for the respectable and quite serious literary tradition founded by Dashiell Hammett.

In certain ways, Hammett's heroes, too, are reminiscent of the unreconstructed Darwinian men. But no matter how rough and appetent they may be, true representative of a rough and appetent society, they are never allowed to run rampant. The author criticizes them. His prose ironizes them, far more astringently then the Kipling man is ironized by a Hemingway, or the D. H. Lawrence man by a Steinbeck. Hammett is, in his less romantic moments, a close and severe critic of the two-fisted red-blooded male whom he derived from tradition and observation. In one of his earliest stories, first published in Mencken's *Smart Set,* he deals with a huge bearded brute of a man who might be a parody of the Hemingway hero, except that he is pre-Hemingway. This impressive bully is much attached to his beard. To make a short story shorter, it turns out that he uses his beard to hide a receding chin. Without the beard, he becomes a laughing stock, a shorn Samson. This isn't much more than farcical anecdote, but it indicates Hammett's attitude towards the half-evolved frontier male of our not too distant past. Shorn and urbanized, he becomes (in Hammett's best novels) a near-tragic figure, a lonely and suspicious alien who pits a despairing and obstinate animal courage against the metropolitan jungle, a not very moral man who clings with desperation to a code of behavior empirically arrived at.

Like the relation of Dickens and Collins the Hemingway-Hammett influence runs two ways. But Hammett does what Hemingway never attempted. He places his characters in complex situations, in great cities like San Francisco and New York and Baltimore, and allows them to work out their dubious salvations under social and economic and political pressures. His subject, you might say, is the frontier male thrust suddenly into the modern megalopolis, as Hemingway's is the same man meeting war and women, and listening to the silence of his own soul. Hammett's prose is not quite a prose that can say anything, as Chandler overenthusiastically claimed it could, but it is a useful prose, with a remarkable range. I dwell on prose for a moment, because a writer's prose really gives us the shape of his talent; his style is the microcosm of his vision. Hammett's prose has pace and point, strong tactile values, the rhythms and colors of speech in the colloquial tradition of Mark Twain and Stephen Crane and H. L. Mencken. It even has some passion, restrained by the doubts and ironies of a good sardonic mind. But it is a deadpan and external prose, artificial-seeming compared with Huck Finn's earthy rhetoric, flat and wooden in comparison with Fitzgerald's instrument. Though it has lyric moments and symbolic overtones, Hammett's prose never attempts the depths of feeling that Hemingway does at his best. Analysis of any kind is alien to it. Molding the surface of things, it lends itself to the vivid narration of rapid, startling action, and is almost perfect for this purpose. But it tends to set too great a premium on action, as if the mind behind it were hurrying away from itself and deliberately restricting itself to the manipulation of appearances. This prose is the expression of that universally-met-with American type who pretends that sensibility and introspection and sentiment are sissified, because he cannot yet cope with the full implications of civilization. James Cain said somewhere that his own discovery of the western roughneck and his attitude made writing possible for him. At its worst such prose seems a phony and unnecessary writing-down to the lowest common denominator of the democracy. But at its best it has great litotic power, in Hemingway's earlier work, or in the fine chapter where Sam Spade makes unspoken love to Brigid by telling her the story of Flitcraft.

Sam Spade is Flitcraft's spiritual twin, the lonely male who is not at ease in Zenith. He is inarticulate about himself, like Babbitt; is aware only of a deep malaise which spurs him on to action and acquisition. *The Maltese Falcon* is a fable of modern man in quest of love and money. Its murders are more or less incidental, though they help to give it its quality of a crime novel, whose characters act out of the extreme emotions of fear and guilt and concupiscence, anger and revenge. Driven by all of these—the Hammett hero is no self-righteous moral playboy, at least until *The Man*—Sam Spade strips away, one by one, the appearances which stand between him and the truth, or between him and the satisfaction of his desires. His story ends with the all-but-complete frustration of his desires. His lover is guilty of murder; the code without which his life is meaningless forces him to turn her over to the police. The black bird is hollow. As in the later novels of Wyndham Lewis, *Revenge for Love* for instance, the reality behind appearances is practically a vacuum. Spade turns for sardonic consolation, one presumes, to the wife of his murdered partner, whose name is Archer. It is his final reluctant act of animal pragmatism.

Probably Hammett intended the ultimate worthlessness of the black bird to be more than a bad joke on his protagonist. I see it as a symbol of a lost tradition. It represents religion and the great cultures of the Mediterranean past which are inaccessible to Spade. Its loss sets a final seal on the inadequacy and superficiality of Spade's life. If only his struggle for self-awareness were more fully realized, his guilt not left unspoken, the stakes for which he struggles not so arbitrarily lost from the beginning, Sam Spade could have been an indigenous tragic figure. As it is, this novel has astonishing imaginative energy after one-third of a century. It can still express contemporary truth, and comes close to tragedy, if there can be such a thing as deadpan tragedy.

* * *

Perhaps I have laid too great stress on the mystery form as psychological symbol and expression. Such lack of proportion, if that is what it is, is a modern common fault among those who studied under Coleridge, and were frightened by Freud and soothed by Jung in their intellectual cradles. I still believe that the subject of most modern novels including mystery novels is psychological truth in the widest sense, expressed more or less symbolically; and that social truth is best revealed by the novelist through individual characters and their conflicts. At the risk of breaking through this thin ice and drowning in deep water, I would even suggest tht the mystery convention is itself a psychological and philosophic symbol. Our best Western minds since Locke and Berkeley and Kant have been concerned with the problem of distinguishing reality from appearance. The modern man is plagued with too much knowledge. We are all Hamlets in a way. (Hamlet, incidentally, was not only the first modern man, but one of the first examples of the hero-as-investigator.) Assailed by conflicting evidence from science, art, religion, common sense, introspection and newspaper headlines, and in default of the traditional rules of evidence, we are in constant danger of not knowing reality when we see it, and bearing false witness to ourselves. The mystery dramatizes this problem for us, and solves it, if not finally, over and over again. Its structural convention requires the probing of appearances for an underlying reality. But there is more to the problem and its solution, as *Hamlet* can teach us, than the triumph of abstract truth and unilateral virtue over outlaw evil. The mystery's traditional answers are too easy, and fail to reach the heart of the old dilemma. I should like to see its philosophic possibilities explored, as Pirandello developed the problem drama for philosophic purpoes, or Kafka the psychological novel for theological ends. The very element of mystification which limits the mystery novel's capacity could perhaps be used, in the hands of an American Dostoevsky, to construct a true imitation of the unsure modern mind and its deceptive world. In such a book a modern man, deeply involved with life, might seek its truth and the truth of himself behind a variety of social and psychological appearances. His truth might be made to penetrate the excessive thinginess of the mystery form and the society it reflects, and accompany all the stages of his quest. It might be a multiple William-Jamesian truth, hidden or half-expressed in the stages of his quest. It might turn out that there is no final truth, that the meaning of the quest, as Justice Holmes once said, is in the quest itself. It could even be that the hero, in seeking for the face of guilt behind the forms of society, might discover with Oedipus that the face of guilt is his very own.

A number of mystery novelists and novelists of suspense, including myself, have taken a leaf from Sophocles's book and bent the mystery into that circular pattern. Mr. Malcolm Cowley writes in a recent *Harper's Magazine* that this pattern of guilty self-discovery is one of the commonest in the contemporary novel. A beautiful example of it is the serious novel, one of the very best we have, Allan Seger's recent *Amos Berry.* Its prevalence reflects our growing ethical self-concern, an attempt to integrate the divided man and the divided responsibility of our Cartesian epoch. I think the most powerful efforts to this end, with all due respect to Sartre and Wyndham Lewis and Moravia, are being and will be made in the United States. After the gay and irresponsible twenties adolescence of our society and its hangover in the thirties and forties, we are no longer content with an easy pharisaism. We are willing to accept responsibility and its attendant pains, responsibility for what happens to us and even for what happens to other people. We are no longer spiritual colonials or provincials dependent on other men's experience for our knowledge of the world and of ourselves. The novels of Faulkner, for instance, *Sanctuary* or *Intruder in the Dust,* even the unsuccessful *Requiem for a Nun,* are bold attempts to face up to a guilt both sectional and national, by implication international too. Such books take up, not the white man's burden, that knapsack filled with contraband, but the burden of civilization, which requires us to know and judge ourselves. As we become custodians of the human conscience, it is scarcely surprising that self-examination and self-inculpation are the theme of so much modern American writing from Hawthorne and Poe to Faulkner and Nelson Algren. On the lower level, the mystery novel which deals honestly with private and public evil, carries this theme to a mass audience. The hero as super-investigator, Sherlock Holmes, never went beyond the rather complacent and patronizing: There, but for the grace of God, go I. There is more humility and redemptive virtue in the contemporary hero-as-defendant, who says: There go I, in spite of the grace of God.

FAREWELL, CHANDLER

Editor's note: "Farewell, Chandler" was, in its original form, a letter written by Ross Macdonald to his publisher, Alfred A. Knopf in 1952.

Ross Macdonald

Farewell, Chandler

Your letter is a hard one to answer. I'll do my best to answer it as well and candidly as I can, even though that will probably require me to discuss myself and my work in what may seem to be an immodest fashion. First of all, I agree with everything that Pocket Books says, except that I seriously doubt the competence of any expert to revise the book for the better. I don't mean that it can't be improved, or that I'm not open to editorial suggestions for rewriting. I am. But I question the point of view from which Pocket Books would like to see the book revised, and I question it on a number of grounds. Their assumption seems to be that my work in general, and this book in particular, is an imitation of Chandler which fails for some reason to come off. Granting that I owe a lot to Chandler, and to Hammett, I have never been a slavish disciple of either. Though I lack Hammett's genius and the intensity which Chandler sustained in his first four novels, I am not wasting my time trying to be one or the other. I am interested in doing things which neither of them was able or willing to do. Let us say that Hammett's subject was the conflict of powerful amoral forces in a money society. (You see, I take Hammett seriously. I think he is a better and more original writer than Steinbeck, for example, and will last longer.) Let us say that Chandler's subject is the evilness of evil, and his highest achievement, the vivid scene of conflict between (conventional) evil and (what he takes to be) good. His unit is the scene, and his overall plots are generally helter-skelter and based on the tired device of blackmail. For that and other reasons, I can't possibly accept Pocket

Books' notion that Chandler is the last word in the mystery or that I differ from him only to err. With all due respect for his power, which I am willing to admit I do not match, but which I also insist I do not try to duplicate, I can't accept Chandler's vision of good and evil. It seems to me that it is conventional to the point of old-maidishness, that it is anti-human to the point of sadism (Chandler hates all women, and really likes only old men, boys, and his Marlow *persona*), and that the mind behind it, for all its tremendous imaginative force, is both uncultivated and second-rate. Since my own mind is neither, it would be simple self-stultification for me to take Chandler as my model and arbiter. His fifth novel is his own self-parody and criticism, clearly displaying the inherent corruption of his view.

My subject is human error. My interest is the exploration of lives. As Pocket Books points out, my stories lack a powerful contrast between good and evil, because I don't see things that way. I did, partly, when I wrote *Blue City*; it was about a town where I had suffered, and several of the characters were based on people I hated. But even the murderers in the last five books have seemed more human than "bad" to me. I would rather understand them than condemn them. I would rather display them in characteristic postures and sum up their lives and the reasons for their lives than cause a self-righteous hero to denounce them or push them around for the sake of action. Because my theme is exploitation rather than conflict, my fables lack punch. But it would spoil them in my eyes to superadd punch. My whole structure is set up to throw insight into lives, not undramatically I hope; its background is psychological and sociological rather than theological. I suppose you could ask whether I should be writing mysteries at all. The answer is that I have been writing mysteries which are good in the opinion of the critics and my colleagues, not so good as Chandler's perhaps and certainly not so popular, but my own. I have been using the form for my own purposes, as any good writer has to use his form. My hope has been to write "popular" novels which would not be inferior to "serious" novels. As I said, I have barely started.

I chose the "hardboiled" form in the first place because it offered both a market and a convention or structure with which almost anything could be done, a technique both difficult and free, and adapted to the subject matter I am interested in. But I have been doing my best to improve the form, and to write real novels in it.

I'm not exactly a money writer, and think I discern in myself the potentiality of first-rate work, and because I take the mystery seriously as a form of the novel, I couldn't very well let Pocket Books tell me what to write or how to write it. Though I admire their incomes, I have no respect for most of the mystery writers they reprint. Furthermore I have a notion that in spite of the Spillane phenomenon which hasn't much to do with the mystery as such but which probably has a lot to do with paperback publishers' notions of what a good mystery should be—the future of the mystery is in the hands of a few good writers. The old-line hardboiled mystery, with many guns and fists and fornications, has been ruined by its own practitioners, including Chandler. Spillane pulled the plug. I refuse to follow it down the drain, because I'm thoroughly convinced that I'm writing something better. That is what my taste and judgment tell me. I can't afford to abdicate them. If I did, I would have to give up my serious literary and novelistic intentions and write for the slick magazines. I've only tried to write one slick story. It sold. I used the $3500 to finance my doctorate.

If I puzzle Pocket Books, Pocket Books also puzzles me when they seem to take it for granted that the new book is a hardboiled mystery, or my idea of a hardboiled mystery. It isn't. Of course it is a variation or offspring of the hardboiled form, but what distinguishes it from the run-of-the-mill hardboiled mystery is the very tone (which I've tried to make literate, humane and, let us face it, adult) to which they object. I can write an ordinary hardboiled mystery with all sorts of shenanigans and gunplay with my eyes closed. I've spent several years developing a form of my own. To jazz it up would be unfortunate, according to my lights, and I seriously doubt if that would make it more saleable. If I can trust my own ear as representative—and I always have trusted my own ear—the public ear may be getting tired of jazzy effects. I expect an audience for my attempt to combine the "popular" and the "sensitive" hero, and to forge a style which combines literacy and flexibility with the virtues of the American—colorful—colloquial. Am I optimistic in thinking that the popular audience is growing up?

Now this may seem an exaggerated and swell-headed response to a perfectly just criticism. Compared with Chandler, my book is lacking in some of the more obvious forms of excitement. My murders are few and offstage. There are no gangsters. My main villains are a pathetic old psychoneurotic and a trapped housewife. My heroine gets upset and makes mistakes. My hero is sexually diffident, ill-paid, and not very sure of himself. Compared with Chandler's brilliant phantasmagoria this world is pale, I agree. But what is the point of comparison? This is not a Chandler book. The characters are less remarkable but more lifelike, for example, and the reader gets to know them better. None of my scenes have ever been written before, and some of them have real depth and moral excitement. I venture to say that none of my characters are familiar; they are freshly conceived from a point of view that rejects black and white classification. There is none, or a good deal less, of the Chandler phoniness. The plot makes sense, and could actually have happened. I could go on for pages. I already have.

I repeat, though, that I know the book is improvable. Any book is, at least any book of mine. If anyone has any ideas about how to give it more speed or power or vividness, without sacrificing the values it already has for me, I'll be glad to go to work on them. My sole objection is to the idea that it is a hardboiled story which misses fire. I'll see if I can write a jacket description as you suggest. And of course I'll have all these things in mind as I write the new book coming up. My main intention in this letter has been to assure you that I know what I'm doing and fully except to be going strong twenty books from now. I couldn't possibly feel that way if I placed my standards outside my own judgment. But on the other hand I'm eager to make a living. Between Spillane and Charybdis is where I am.

What is Pocket Books so worried about? Lee Wright herself (along with various other connoisseurs) named *Moving Target* as the best American non-Simon and Schuster mystery of its year. With the exception of *Drowning Pool,* my books since *Target* have been getting better. Any mystery writer can be made to look bad by comparing him with Chandler, *from Chandler's point of view.* After all Chandler is universally recognized as the American master of the mystery story, along with Hammett (though I think the latter is far and away the more important writer). I'd prefer to be compared with the current crop. And please give me a little more time. Chandler had been writing for at least fifteen years before I ever thought of writing a mystery, and I turned professional just six years ago. My peak is still coming, and I've yet to find the form that suits my talent. I only know it isn't behind me.

Still, I'm willing to bet that Pocket Books will have to order a second printing of *The Way Some People Die.* In spite of its dismal record in hard cover, I'm convinced that it can be sold in paper. If it fails, I'll be in a mood to write you a *Dark Blue City. Blue City,* by the way, took exactly two months and I wrote two other books the same year.

I have no objections to *The Convenient Corpse* as a title, though it doesn't exactly jar me all the way down to my heels. It's a nice neat ordinary title. By all means use it, though I don't quite catch its relevance to the book; that doesn't matter. What do you think of *The Sinister Habit*? It's a phrase from Cocteau, the reference being to "the sinister habit of asking questions."

Well, I've written more than I intended to, let my hair down in fact. I hope I haven't labored *my* point of view. If I turn out to be Athanasius against the world, I'll rewrite places where the story drags or characters fade out. Show me the places. I certainly don't think the whole book needs rewriting. It's already had a lot of it. Don't you think it's a good well-placed story as it stands, and that perhaps a main difficulty comes from pigeon-holing it as a hardboiled item? While no one would mistake it for a *major opus,* I must confess I was pleased with the characterization—the characters seemed more human than in anything I've done, closer to life—and more than pleased with the plot. The trouble with a highly organized plot, such as I have a predilection for, is that it determines and controls the movement of the story. I know I have a tendency to underplay the individual scenes, to make the book the unit of effect. Chandler practices, and has stated, the opposite theory: that a good plot is one that makes good scenes. I don't wish to give the impression that he's my *bête noire.* Hell, he's one of my masters. But I can see around him, and am in growing disagreement with much of his theory and practice. That is why the present book, which is more different from Chandler and more like myself than any of the other Macdonald books, is important to me, and why I have set out my ideas about Chandler at such length. As I see it, my hope of real success as a writer, both artistic and commercial, resides in developing my own point of view and craft and technique to the limit. Chandler had something to say or tell, and said it powerfully. I have something different to say, about similar subjects and the same society. The satisfaction of saying it and the hope of saying it better are more important to me than my status as a commercial artist would seem to warrant. But if I overvalue my work, that is the defect of the virtue of believing in what I am doing. My peculiar ability to take the mystery as a serious form is half my strength as a mystery writer. I only wish *The Convenient Corpse* were a better example of what I am talking about. Now it's up to me to write one.

I'd rather do that than rewrite the book that I have just finished writing and rewriting. My standards are high even though they may be mistaken, and I never let a book out of my hands until I've given it everything that I happen at the moment to have. One of my obvious problems, though, is doing a first-rate job on a book which will ultimately bring me about three thousand dollars, which is scarcely enough to live on for six months. *If* Pocket Books decides to take it—is that the question at stake? I realize, of course, that your and Pocket Books' intention is to find ways and means of improving sales and incidentally my income. In the light of that, I hope my counter assertion doesn't sound churlish. I suppose I was a little startled by the suggestion that experts might sharpen my book up for me. If any rewriting has to be done, I feel I must do it myself. Revision by persons other than the writer might possibly work for a book, but it cannot work for a writer. That is why Hollywood writers lose their morals so quickly and their writing ability eventually, and why movies in general are so bad. A writer has to defend his feeling of free and joyful creation, illusory as it may be, and his sense that what he is writing is his own work.

Margaret Millar

Highlights

People who knew the quiet shy man who was my husband will be surprised to learn the contents of our first conversation. We had gone to high school together, even shared some of the same classes, but it was years after graduation before we actually talked. We met on a street in London, Ontario. Characteristically, Ken was carrying an armful of books. Uncharacteristically, he said he was on his way to Ireland and invited me to go with him. Fast work for a slow mover. It wasn't, in fact, all that fast. His best friend told me years later that Ken said he intended to marry me. Ken's age at the time was fifteen.

The invitation to Ireland both shocked and flattered me. Of course I had to turn it down. Nice Canadian girls didn't go to Ireland on the first date.

I received a couple of letters from Ken during the following year, one from Ireland where he was visiting an aunt, the other from Scotland where he was about to start a bicycle trip from Edinburgh to London.

Then, in 1936, I was in the Public Library in London, Ontario, translating Xenophon, which is easy Greek and allows the attention to wander. Mine wandered to the front desk where a handsome young man was checking out a pile of books a yard high. I walked up behind him and said, "Where did you leave your bicycle?"

Books have been the basis of our life together. Ken was carrying an armful of books when we met on the street in London, and there he was a year later loading up again in the library. He carried books almost to the end. He liked to hold them in his hands, to move them from place to place, to take them out of one drawer and put them in another.

A relationship as lasting as ours had many unforgettable highlights, beginning with the invitation to Ireland. The last occurred a few weeks before he died. I had, with the aid of our friend, Jorge Gamio, taken Ken down to the beach club for a swim. The sea seemed almost as natural an environment for Ken as it does for the sealions which occasionally swam alongside him. That day he swam in the pool because severe winter storms had denuded the beach of sand. Pool or sea, water invigorated him. He came up to the cabana where I was waiting.

"Hi Maggie," he said. "You're looking wonderful."

This might not seem much of a highlight except that this was the first time in six months he had recognized me. The moment of recognition passed and his face went blank again. I will remember it for the rest of my life.

Robert Easton

A Quiet Man

"Ken didn't mind silence," our mutual friend Noel Young observed. I concurred; Ken's writing rings with silence—the implications of words said or unsaid. So did his personal presence. I didn't know this at first.

We met in the early '50s at a gathering of what was and remains known as the Santa Barbara Writers' Luncheon. All of us fitted into one booth at Harry's Cafe on lower State Street. There were Young, now a leading California publisher; Willard Temple, whose stories were appearing in *Collier's* and *Saturday Evening Post;* William Campbell Gault, a Dutton author of sport and mystery novels; versatile Dennis Lynds, better known now under his pen name of Michael Collins; and our gray eminence Paul Ellerbe, a popular short story pro who retired to Santa Barbara to die but was going strong at seventy-four.

It wasn't a Bohemian hideout—no such thing existed in Santa Barbara in those days—but a popular stop for business and professional types, shoppers, tourists. Ken could have been mistaken for a Rotarian in coat and tie.

He was my height, five eleven, but much heavier, nearly 200 pounds, solid, with that deceptively babyface look some very intelligent people have; so reserved he seemed rude. I couldn't remember anyone being so uncommunicative at a social occasion. Yet when a topic came up which appealed to him he spoke out tersely with complete assurance straight to the point, often with remarkable erudition.

I thought I detected flashes of warmth beneath his cool blue-eyed reticence but had no idea they included me until several months later when we happened to meet on the street. Ken greeted me with surprising cordiality. Suddenly he asked if I'd like to go sailing. I hadn't planned to but it was a fine day and I wanted to respond to his friendliness. I thought from the way he spoke he must own his own boat and use it regularly.

At the harbor I was surprised when he suggested we rent a knockabout and share the cost. I'm a landsman, know little about the water, but went along with a secure feeling I was in experienced hands.

Ken silently took the tiller and directed me how to manage the ropes which controlled the boom of the single sail. Tacking seaward a couple of miles, we looked back at that breathtaking panorama of beaches, mission towers, foothills with their red-tiled houses, and backdrop of steep mountains which is Santa Barbara.

We'd said almost nothing. Instead there was that quiet intimacy of shared function, thought, being. His reticence was, I realized, entirely natural. When words seemed necessary he used them; otherwise, silence. Neither of us suspected we were inaugurating a relationship pattern which would continue thirty years.

In due course I learned that though Ken was to some extent familiar with boats, he'd never taken such a sail before. It was simply a case of his deciding to do something and doing it—with the ulterior motive of getting to know me better.

Our friendship ripened through those biweekly writers' luncheons. They were almost the only social contacts Ken had during an intensely stressful period when he was producing a novel a year in order to survive. These were of course not potboilers but the beginnings of a body of work which would be recognized as the finest of its kind. His wife Margaret was producing novels of similarly high quality. Ken told me their combined income was about what a high school teacher earned.

To supplement their income he began teaching a creative writing course at night at the Santa Barbara Adult Education Center. Ken had taught before turning to writing full time and retained strong leanings toward the profession. Now he chaired writers' conferences sponsored by Adult Ed. and at his invitation I joined him on discussion panels where I became aware of his deep understanding of books and writers and his ability to communicate it. Without flaunting his Phi Beta Kappa key or his doctorate from Michigan, he was at home with Greek and Roman classics, and familiar with American and European writing as well as England's. He cherished a special liking for Russian fiction. Appropriately, the Russians would find a special liking for his; he later became popular there.

The breadth of his current reading astonished me. It included history, biography, poetry, a great deal of literary criticism (since undergraduate days he'd reviewed books for pleasure and pay and considered criticism an important aspect of writing) and many social issues such as racism, poverty, and crime.

His mentors as a writer, he told me, were Coleridge, that pioneer explorer of the darker side of human psychology, Wilkie Collins, Dickens, Fitzgerald, and of course Hammett and Chandler. He particularly mentioned the social concerns of Collins and Dickens. His own writing expressed similar concerns though I'd not yet discovered all the reasons for them.

We discussed at length the talking voice or appropriate tone—that attitude toward subject matter which, we decided, a beginning writer always hears from some source outside himself, whether from reading or actual life, and adapts as his own. Ken said he first heard it unforgettably in James M. Cain's tough but tender *The Postman Always Rings Twice*. "You can say anything with a voice like that."

He was proud of being a popular writer like Cain, had no desire to be what he called "a mandarin like Joyce or Beckett" though he appreciated them. He felt strongly that his voice, his work—he himself—belonged at popular level.

Audiences quickly penetrated his often crusty reserve to the wisdom and caring below, where there was also a store of shyness and gentleness.

When age finally overtook Paul Ellerbe, Ken assumed leadership of our luncheon group and asked if I thought we should continue to meet every two weeks. I suggested once a month, but he continued it biweekly. I sensed he felt anything less frequent would represent a kind of retreat, a lessening of our loyalty to each other and to writing. He personally telephoned each of us—we numbered more than a dozen now, so it was no little chore—to alert and invite us. Yet at lunch he would say little unless a topic initiated by someone else appealed to him. In conversation as in writing he was usually a counterpuncher—responding to leads of others—like those cases others brought before his fictional alter ego Lew Archer. Ken would then proceed to sort out essentials, and usually reached the heart of the matter.

His reticence was also, I realized, a form of conservation of energy. His time and strength were limited; he wanted to make the most of them.

Though a liberal in politics and a fiery sympathizer with underdogs and minorities, Ken was a conservative in almost everything else: clothes (the coat and tie were true symbols—he usually bought them at Penney's), short hair, food (he ate anything but preferred meat and potatoes), lifestyle generally, even his writing. If you listen to those reverberating silences which surround his words, the moral conservative can be heard, saying in effect that life is beautiful and dangerous and we'd better be careful with it.

I discovered too that Ken cherished a strong conviction that Santa Barbara should be the center for writing and the other arts it has since become. He had an almost Athenian sense of self in relation to the community, of community as an extension of self, state as an extension of community. It was one reason he chaired those early conferences and became our group leader. Similar concern led him to serve on a citizen committee investigating the cause of a bloody riot at our campus of the University of California, and to become a working trustee of our natural history museum, and much more.

Ken arrived here under special circumstances. In 1944 after seeing him off at San Diego as an officer aboard an aircraft carrier, Margaret passed through on the train en route to their home in Canada. Glancing out the window she was so struck by what she saw that she got off at the next station and took the next train back to Santa Barbara, found a four-room house on unfashionable Bath Street, bought it and was waiting there with their young daughter Linda when Ken returned after the war. He fell in love with the community at first sight as she had done. I'd grown up here feeling much the same way; it brought us together on particularly personal ground.

During our walks and talks—sometimes along the beach, his second habitat, sometimes on Mountain Drive bordering the foothills, mine—Ken told me of his painful childhood and youth. He'd been born near San Francisco in 1915, the same year I was born there. It gave us a further bond and Ken a joint U.S.-Canadian identity of which he was proud. Both his parents were Canadians, his father a harbor-boat captain, his mother a nurse. Earlier John Macdonald

Millar had been a newspaper editor, read widely, written poetry, ventured off into Canada's northern regions to live with Indians—been drawn romantically to Far North and Far West as many were in the early years of this century.

The family was happy at first. Ken recalled joyful moments standing beside his father at the wheels of harbor boats. Then one day in Vancouver his father abandoned him and his mother, leaving them penniless in a waterfront boarding house. Ken remembered begging for money and food on the streets at the age of six.

By the time he was sixteen he could count fifty different rooms he'd lived in. Once, his nearly desperate mother, feeling unable to care for him properly, took him as far as the gates of an orphanage, resolved to give him up, but changed her mind.

Ken never forgot those gates. Much of his writing was, I think, consciously or subconsciously an exorcism of the terrible bitterness and resentment and loneliness and lack of status of those early years. They also gave him an embracing social concern, plus that fiery sympathy for underdogs.

While he was in high school in Kitchener, Ontario, already admiring Margaret, the mayor's daughter and brightest girl in his class, his father, broken and dying, was in the city's charity hospital. His father's final condition and presence were further embarrassment, a grim reminder Ken found hard to accept though he and his mother did what they could to help. "He'd condemned me to a life of emotional deprivation and humiliating poverty."

Many of Ken's novels revolve around the search for a true father. He could neither forgive nor forget his actual one.

A few years later while attending college at the University of Western Ontario, still living with his mother, he came home from class one afternoon and found her dead on the bathroom floor from a massive cerebral hemorrhage. Ken's early years were not happy ones.

There was a dourness and violence in him which I think stemmed largely from them. He was often quick to take offense, irascible, lashing out at injustices real or imaginary.

His fictional villains are often the rich and powerful who fail to act responsibly toward those less fortunate—among whom he numbered himself. To survive as the person he wanted to be he'd been obliged to develop a powerful ego, positive opinions which sometimes became overbearing.

It was as if there were two Kens: one in whom violence and darkness seethed, one yearning for tenderness and light. "I'm a depressed person!" he confessed on several occasions. Then I sensed the near-presence of that sensitive waif who'd lived in fifty different rooms obliged to accept the charity of others, ever mindful of orphanage gates and his absent father.

Our association as activists in a common cause began with efforts to protect the endangered California condor. Ken and Margaret were ardent birders and had recently led in organizing the Santa Barbara Audubon Society. Its 700 members in a community of some 70,000 testified to their organizational abilities. My association with the condor went back to the 1930s when I'd helped establish a condor refuge in our wild Santa Barbara back country.

The condor issue boiled up this time over a Forest Service proposal to build roads into the condors' habitat and to allow off-road vehicles in wild areas. There were hearings, phone calls, committee meetings, letters to editors and politicians. It was our introduction to the trench warfare of what was becoming known as the conservation movement.

Ken wrote a hard-hitting article for *Sports Illustrated* which presented our local issues to a national audience and brought us widespread support. I co-authored a book titled *California Condor* and Ken arranged for Brooks Atkinson, former drama critic of the *New York Times,* then its roving columnist and a dedicated bird lover, to write the introduction.

Underlying our activism was a growing feeling that the earth and its wild creatures have rights of their own much as people do, not to mention their value to humans when permitted to exist in their natural state. "The condor," Ken wrote, "is our canary in the mine—the mine slowly filling with pollutants which is a possible image of our world—and if the condor survives, perhaps we may too."

These efforts merged into a larger one for which the condor became a symbol: creation of a 142,000-acre wilderness area—the first established under the Wilderness Act of 1964—which protected both condor and wilderness. Meanwhile Ken finished his next book *The Instant Enemy* and asked me to read the manuscript. I protested that I seldom read mystery novels and might not be much help. "No," he contradicted, "you'll come to it with a fresh mind!" I was astonished by the finished quality of his manuscript. Aside from a typographical error or two and an occasional change of diction, there were few suggestions I could make.

He told me he wrote—not merely planned but wrote—his books in his head before he sat down to write them on paper.

To produce 300 or 400 pages of such finished work in about 365 days seemed to me an extraordinary achievement—the more so since my own books were quite different, each feeling its way in a new direction toward a general audience. I think this diversity interested Ken. It challenged his problem-solving talents. His help was invaluable. Perhaps the sagest advice he gave me was the simplest: "There's a way to say everything!"

For nearly twenty years we read and criticized each other's work regularly before publication. I seldom found his judgment wrong. Once after going against it I worked two years on a novel which finally had to be shelved. Ken just grinned. "I've got one on the shelf too! What writer hasn't?"

His was an early autobiographical one done before he realized he couldn't deal directly with "the radioactive materials of my own life"—also before he understood that to survive financially he must adopt a genre such as the mystery and become proficient at it. What convinced him, he said, was a general-interest story which took three months to write and three more to sell—for $300.

What brought us closer than anything before was our teenage daughters. Ken's was the same age as one of mine. They were experiencing similar emotional problems.

When Ken was hospitalized partly as a result of trying to cope with Linda's problems, I was able to help. When my wife and I reached our wits' end, Ken's and Margaret's support was invaluable. Ken wrote later in one of his novels: "The moral beatings people took from their children, I was thinking, were the hardest to endure and the hardest to escape." Our daughters might have said the same in reverse about us but it did not ease the pain we shared.

Ken's health was seriously undermined by his difficulties with Linda and added to the enormous strain of producing a novel annually. I thought he might never leave the hospital: hypertension, heart trouble, gout. But he fought back gallantly. Soon he was swimming his regular half mile and attempting our old walks. He'd been a wrestler in college; physical aptitude was an important aspect of his existence. At first our walks were a few hundred yards. Gradually they increased to three miles.

He was taking nine different medications daily, he told me. He used a new drug which kept him from being condemned to a wheelchair by gout. Ken was as determined not to be an invalid as he was determined to write well.

Big success came in 1969 with *The Goodbye Look.* Rave reviews. Sales of tens of thousands in hardcover. Alfred Knopf himself wrote the copy for the large advertisement which appeared in the *New York Times* in company with Ken's photo, also by Knopf. Knopf audaciously advised *Times* readers that *Ada* (Nabokov's current bestseller) could wait while they read Ken. Ken had gone to Knopf originally, he told me, "because I thought him the best publisher in the country. He didn't know me from Adam. I sent him a manuscript. He accepted it." Now their relationship was paying off. Sales of movie and television rights followed.

Ken smiled more after that. It was about the only outward difference fame made in him. In fact a near-lifetime of struggle for personal identity, professional recognition, and financial security was ended. He and Margaret bought a larger house in the exclusive suburb of Hope Ranch, not because of its exclusiveness but because it had more room and quiet than their earlier quarters near the foothills. "And so that I'd have to keep working to pay for it!" Like Goethe's Faust, Ken was not one to rest on beds of ease, and like Goethe he was obliged to struggle daily against his inner darkness. Writing was his ladder toward the light.

The Goodbye Look appeared just as an event occurred which irrevocably changed his beloved Santa Barbara, and mine. At midafternoon on January 29, 1969 my telephone rang. Ken's usually quiet voice sounded excited. "There's a report of a big oil spill off shore. Have you heard?" I hadn't.

The evening paper headlined the shocking news. An oil well five miles off our waterfront had "blown out." A black tide was spreading.

Walking on Mountain Drive overlooking the city Ken and I brooded over the sight and its implications. "The odor of crude oil reached us like the whiff of a decaying future," Ken wrote later. "It seemed to us that if the spill had meaning, that meaning would have to be created by the people on the scene." Thousands of seabirds died. Commercial fishing and pleasure boating came to a complete halt. Tourism declined sharply. The quality of human life over a wide area was threatened.

We joined dozens of other citizens in the picket line at city-owned Stearns Wharf, a loading and unloading point for craft supplying the offshore platforms. Somehow this black disaster must be converted into a turning point, a signpost marking the end of such ruinous environmental carelessness.

To gather firsthand information for articles and books, Ken and Margaret and I flew over the great oil slick which now covered some 1,200 square miles. We watched its tentacles spreading like those of a black octopus up and down the coast and out between the Channel Islands as far seaward as we could see.

Such efforts, in company with widespread media coverage and my later book for which Ken did the introduction, helped make the spill a national event and triggered what became known as the environmental movement.

Attitudes changed. Things would never be the same again. One result was the passage by Congress of the environmental protection act, the national air quality and clean water acts, as well as numerous tightenings of state and federal regulations concerning offshore drilling. Santa Barbara became a center for the environmental movement and Ken one of its recognized spokesmen.

He decided to put the oil spill into fiction as he and I had put it into fact. "I think I'll make this the first environmental mystery novel." *Sleeping Beauty* concerns a thinly disguised version of the Santa Barbara spill. It may indeed be the first ecological mystery. It also memorialized Ken's only child. Linda had died, tragically young, of a cerebral hemorrhage. Transfigured, she is the sleeping beauty of this in many ways most tender of Ken's books.

When I read the manuscript of Ken's last novel *The Blue Hammer* I sensed a lessening of tension. I mentioned it as part of my usual criticism. He answered that it was deliberate. "I want to be a little mellower, a little more tolerant with this one." Yet I sensed something more: a lessening of that masterful grip which characterized earlier work. Alzheimer's disease, beginning subtly, was probably the cause, I realized later.

A contributing factor was undoubtedly the screenplay. Ken vowed repeatedly he would never write for Hollywood. He believed it had destroyed the talent of one of his most admired models, Fitzgerald. He'd refused handsome offers. But this project, appealingly presented by people he liked, intrigued him. "It's a challenge," he told me.

"I want to see if I can do it!" Nothing came of it but money, and mental and physical exhaustion. Ken was left an easy prey to the illness which was stalking him.

Margaret's precarious health compounded his difficulties: cancer from which she recovered, then oncoming blindness which proved irreversible. His concern for her was an aspect of his total concern for all with whom he was intimately associated. But I could tell something more was breaking him down, driving him inward, keeping him—or so it seemed—from undertaking a new book; and finally—as his powers failed—from reading mine in manuscript as he'd done so generously for so many years. "My memory seems to be leaving me," he explained.

I joked that none of us in our sixties was a whiz kid. But he knew he was failing and it increased his withdrawal.

Before he wrote *The Blue Hammer* Ken intimated he was thinking of a new kind of book—"something entirely different; it might not be a Lew Archer novel." At the height of his power, he seemed ready for a new step. After *The Blue Hammer* was in manuscript I asked about the other book. He smiled enigmatically and said he'd changed his mind. Whatever the new step, he never took it.

Ken was the first person I heard use the phrase: "Writing well is the best revenge." He wanted to die in harness as a writer. That wish was not granted. But he has had his revenge.

Hugh Kenner

Learning

"We could make," Ken said in his level Lew Archer voice, "a *Revenge for Love* sandwich." He meant, we could move my discussion of a 1936 novel by Wyndham Lewis into the center of the larger presentation, something unobtrusively three-parted. Parts I and III—the bread—would have humbler business. Ken's novels had often employed "sandwich" chapters, three main scenes with the meaty one in the center, and since the craft I was trying to learn was a kind of narrative his experience had every chance of being helpful. Besides—this would slip out—he was really an academic himself, as it were on extended sabbatical. Some day the Coleridge thesis would be consummated. . . . (And one day it was.)

We had met in 1950 at George Hand's, in a house, on "the Riviera," with a million-dollar view over Santa Barbara's twinkling lights. George Hand, crag-faced, broken-nosed, saturnine, liked to call himself an ex-plumber, alluding to the Great Depression that seemed to hover just behind his gaunt shoulder, as well as to the book on Swift he could neither start nor forget. "A poor boy," was his nostalgic phrase for young Swift. By then a dean at a parvenu U.C. campus, he had afforded that house when academic salaries were meager thanks to a piece of luck Swift would have smiled at: shells from a Japanese sub had crashed on a seaside cactus patch ten miles away, knocking down little save Riviera real estate values. George and his wife Lucy and their daughters entertained there; one of Ken's books is dedicated "To All Hands." (Listening back, I hear a ragtime piano; can it have been George himself who played it?)

So one night some new English faculty members were there, the Kenners among them, and so were Ken and Margaret Millar. Margaret and I shared a U. of Toronto background; that must have been the link in our host's mind. But Margaret at that time, it turned out, did not much care for academics, unless they were into something human like ragtime. What I was into was how writing is done, and it was years before she and I improved on a surface cordiality. Instead Ken and I were the ones who drew towards each other, warily.

We had two things in common: Canadian roots, and, yes, a formal interest in writing. He was monolithic, monosyllabic, contained. I was reticent by temperament, garrulous by impulse. His calm gaze, his cryptic assurance nettled me, yet everything he said bespoke good sense. He said very little indeed. He watched and listened. He liked Faulkner; at that time I didn't. He had begun fiction in frank imitation of Faulkner, in novels published under his own name. It was when he switched styles and personae that he turned into Ross Macdonald. He urged me to read Hammett and Chandler; also a friend of his named Henry Branson

Somehow our shaky acquaintance prospered. One evening in their house on seedy Bath Street (that was before there was any movie money) he showed me translations ("I am a best-seller in France"). Margaret, a world-class best seller, had been translated farther afield: into Swedish for instance. Opened on at random in a book with her name on it, a bizarre sentence abrim with a's turned out to be Swedish for "Canada is teeming with wolves"; the three of us mouthed its syllables in hilarity. But Ken in French—a language I could read—that was an odd revelation. His Faulknerian manner, resembling *littérature,* nestled comfortably into the idiom of Baudelaire, which tells you something about the antecedents of Faulkner. But, translated to the land of Descartes, his Hammett/Chandler (Lew Archer) manner turned ludicrous: short toneless sentences of no distinction, with bits of American, literally transcribed, sticking out of them like technical terms. "Donnez-moi le gat" is not authentic but conveys the effect. Yet the shelf had title after title on display: in France they read "Macdonald" avidly.

What could have mesmerized the fastidious Gauls, from beneath so risible a linguistic surface? Nothing but what their language calls "ordonnance": arrangement: the economical sequencing of effects. *Ordonnance,* that was what this stolid man understood. "Archer is not a writer," he once said of his narrator; certainly Archer was not given to cadenzas or phrasal outbursts: not like the Kenneth Millar of the earliest books. Yet, guiding Archer's pen, a shrewd literary intelligence wasted no moves in the intricate game of expounding Oedipal chess that had run for three generations while the sleuth in the foreground poked about for mere days, a mere 200 pages. Exposition? Those books were *all* exposition; and if what got expounded seemed no more cogent than the binomial theorem—that is how Freud's kinky diagrams strike me still—then the skill thanks to which the exposition held your interest was that much the more marked.

Within months I was bringing him my 20-page drafts that floundered into qualification, to learn the next day how I might restitch them into something that moved; that moreover left the reader clear about what he'd moved through. That was the era of the *Revenge for Love* sandwich. What I'd done with *The Revenge for Love* doesn't matter—scattered my dealings with it, probably. I tended to do that. Ken wanted it grouped, compacted, and made central, to firm up a chapter. However radical, his surgery was always simple, and he could teach the way of it: you worked with blocks, several pages in length—two, three, maybe six blocks per chapter—and you gave thought to their order. The order of blocks was like the sequencing of events in a narrative, and if the first block did some scene setting that was sound. His eye, as it scanned my drafts, was alert for the contours of blocks.

I could not scan them usefully myself. I'd not even known it was narrative I was attempting. Exposition, I had been taught, was one thing, but narrative something else. Ken was quietly persuasive. *All* was narrative. When hard to follow, it was *bad* narrative. Narrative meant no more than serial revelations in time. What did I hope to accomplish, as my reader turned pages? To persuade? Then successful persuasion would be an event, perhaps slow, perhaps dramatic: an event in my reader's mind. Better if I made it a pleasurable event, letting narrative shape its rhythms. And remembering sandwiches.

So, in 1952-3, under Ken Millar's tutelage, I wrote the little book all my subsequent books have derived from: *Wyndham Lewis*, which I'm glad to say is still in print. It begins, "The Wyndham Lewis of subsequent legend . . .", and launches into a story. That was how to hold a reader, always was, and is still.

For a while I brought him everything as I wrote it. Though we disagreed about Freud, he helped me with the review of the Ernest Jones biography that appeared in *The Hudson Review* and later in my book *Gnomon;* he even provided its title: "Tales of the Vienna Woods." He scanned the first versions of my book on Beckett; it was between us that the central "bicycle" chapter came into shape, a chapter Beckett liked.

Now and then our talk affected his work too. Mickey Spillane, then a comet, he abhorred; yet I once suggested that as long as Archer hid behind the first person pronoun, he and Spillane's Mike Hammer were not greatly unlike. That slender pronoun was apt to conceal, I thought, a character slenderly conceived. Ken's right hand crushed a beer can as I talked; then some months later he handed me a new book in typescript. The protagonist was not Archer but a compassionate probation officer, whose quest for justice brought him at one point to the office of a private eye, grungy, unprepossessing. And, said Ken, "That's Archer, seen from the outside." Archer's outside being established, the later books wisely reclaimed the old Archer-centricity.

Altogether, we were close enough to feel strains. What we had in common was little enough: Canada, writing, and a community, academic and civic, about which we seemed to disagree almost continually. George and Lucy Hand died: we lost that link. Moreover politics was Ken's litmus paper, as for a 17th century Englishman religion would have been; he had strong unexpected canons of disapproval, and greatly disapproved of people I came to value.

There was no breach, no, but, enmeshed in personal affairs, we gradually saw less of each other. Nothing more dramatic than my terminated relationship with U.C.S.B. was what finally forced a parting, and a tenuous parting it was. When after 23 years I headed east, we were so little in touch that I did not call on him. But when I drove out of Santa Barbara in 1973 my last stop was Kisch's Books, to buy a little meditation of Ken's, *On Detective Fiction,* and my first act on arriving at Johns Hopkins was to send it to him for inscription. He responded, movingly. He was one of my oldest friends, and of my valued teachers nearly the last to die. An honest writer too. If the new Library of America series survives, it will be thanks to such catholicity of judgment as will, one day, include, next to Melville and Mrs. Stowe, sparsely annotated, on acid-free paper, a triplet by Ross Macdonald: the exact cogs turning in their quiet Rolex way, the twists of idiom measured, the scenes, the little silences, the speed, the parsimony: in short the *ordonnance,* just to teach our posterity.

Julian Symons

A Transatlantic Friendship

"So you've met Ross Macdonald twenty times," somebody said to me once. "Did you get twenty words out of him?" I said truthfully that I'd got many more words than that, but it's true that Ken (it seems right to shift gear into the name by which everybody called him) had no small talk. When something was said to him he would consider it, almost visibly turning over the possible implications of his reply, and when the slow-spoken reply came it would be a genuine expression of feeling about the subject in hand. Such a reaction may sound ponderous, but that wasn't at all the effect. His verbally well-shaped response might be light or serious, but it by-passed the ordinary banalities of conversation. He was quite capable of saying that he had no opinion about the subject, or knew too little about it for anything he said to be worth uttering. Even with people he liked, conversation with Ken Millar could be difficult, but it was never unrewarding. Looking back, I'm doubtful if our meetings numbered twenty but still our friendship, much of it conducted by letters across the Atlantic, was a warm one.

We met first in 1965, at the annual dinner of Mystery Writers of America. His book *The Chill* had won an award from British crime writers which took the form of a dagger, and I had been delegated to hand it over. Ken accepted it, held it aloft, asked: "Is this a dagger that I see before me?" and made a downward plunge in the air. Afterwards he and I found ourselves having drinks at an apartment in the company of Victor and Ruth Gollancz. "Isn't she the most beautiful lady you've ever seen?" he asked when we were walking back to our hotels. Ruth was then I suppose in her mid-sixties, and although her features and coloring were delicate I didn't endorse his remark. He had, as I learned later, a special feeling for beauty and dignity in those who had passed middle age. I was struck at this first meeting by his own good looks, the sweetness of his smile, and by a natural courtesy much beyond the ordinary.

We had arranged, as I thought rather casually, to meet on the following day. At nine o'clock the telephone rang. "That will be Julian," Ken said in his gentle voice, and surprised me by asking how I felt, with the implication that our half-dozen drinks represented a real night out together. Perhaps they may have done for him, since his use of alcohol was very modest. We walked through Central Park, went to the Guggenheim and saw an exhibition that fairly bowled Ken over (German expressionists? Shamefully, infuriatingly, I can't remember), walked downtown talking about modern poetry. In this connection I perpetrated a considerable gaffe when I said something like: "The most important English poetry publishers—I don't suppose you know of them—are Faber and Faber." A pause, a long pause, and then the gentle voice was raised in just indignation. "Not *know* of Faber and Faber. At Ann Arbor, Julian, I took a course with Auden, I made a special study of imagism. I used to *buy* Faber poetry when I was in college. . . ." I apologized and was forgiven, although the rash assumption rankled for a while. Ken's knowledge of poetry was extensive, especially of the nineteenth century romantics who had influenced him in youth. Among modern poets he admired particularly Lowell and Berryman.

From that brief time in New York I carry away also the recollection of his amazement when, at lunch with him and the crime novelist Jean Potts after our Guggenheim visit, I ordered calves' brains. Brains—for lunch—after an evening of excess like ours—Ken did not withhold his wonder, and his admiration of such stamina, such intrepidity.

We met again four years later when Kathleen and Sarah, wife and daughter, came with me on a holiday interspersed with lectures that ordered and shaped our movements. I talked about Wyndham Lewis at the University of California at Santa Barbara, and Ken called to collect us from our motel and take us to their house on Via Esperanza. I knew and admired the crime stories of his wife Margaret Millar, and now met her for the first time. She was breezy where Ken was quiet, apparently as bluffly extrovert as he was inward-looking: yet Margaret had her private demons, expressed by the asthma that made it impossible for her to stay in a smoke-filled room, and the eye trouble that made her reluctant to go out at night. As he played with the dogs in and around the pool, Ken said that I should not be deceived by what might look like luxury. "I make about as much money every year as a good plumber." He had already embarked on the attempt to re-create and understand his own past that increasingly preoccupied him as a novelist, but the immense critical and popular success in America of his later books still lay a year or two ahead. He was less concerned with such things than any writer I have known, taking little interest in sales and promotion, almost none in the films made from his stories.

It turned out that he knew a lot about Wyndham Lewis (I had not repeated my Faberian mistake), and had been friendly with Hugh Kenner who arranged the lecture. This turned out disastrously, thanks to the fact that the room in which it was given had been changed, and the new room number not made public. The audience was even smaller than it might otherwise have been and Ken, who set out to attend the lecture, spent the evening wandering down corridors and through empty classrooms.

A couple of years later the Millars made what was for them the momentous decision in favor of a trip to Europe. Ken had not been in Britain for more than thirty years, and Margaret I think had never crossed the Atlantic. Kathleen and I wanted to give a dinner party for them, and there was also a plan for a radio discussion with them both. Ken wrote:

> If I was dubious, when you were here, about our being able to come to England, it had to do with Margaret's difficulty in traveling and doing the things that people ordinarily and quite easily do. Well, I have got her to the point of abandoning, for a week or two, this continent. But there are still some limitations on our movements. I am being perfectly frank with you and Kathleen because you will understand me. It would be difficult for Margaret to meet any number of people at your house, and indeed it is many years (I think since the inception of her glaucoma, now happily arrested) since she has gone anywhere after dark, even in her own familiar territory. She asks if we could have lunch together, perhaps at a pub, instead? M thrives on informality, as you may have noticed.

The question of coming or not coming to dinner involved a flurry of correspondence, Ken feeling quite mistakenly that what he said above had been impolite. "This self-disinvited guest doesn't seem to know how to handle his social mistake without making the further gaffe of reinviting himself," he wrote. "Conceivably—I blunder on—we might manage to meet at your house and eat somewhere afterward, with or without dear M." He had called Donald Davie at Stanford, asked whom he should see in London, and I had been recommended with "the most outright endorsement of anybody that I ever heard from Davie." But perhaps, he feared, Kathleen and I had given up on the Millars. "That would *really* make me feel badly."

More letters followed, expressing alarm at one moment, eager expectancy the next. All this may sound exaggerated or slightly absurd, but that isn't so. The trip in prospect was both exciting and alarming, with the first true for Ken, the second for Margaret. In the end Ken came alone to dinner with us in Battersea, I later took them both out to lunch, and although the husband-and-wife radio discussion didn't come off, Ken took part in a radio program in which I talked to him about his books. I can't remember much about the dinner, except that he got on extremely well with the crime critic and political commentator Matthew Coady, but otherwise seemed faintly uneasy. I should perhaps have realized that he flourished in a very small group, with more direct and meaningful conversation than a dinner party encourages.

Our lunch date a couple of days later had some touches of comedy about it. I had booked a table at a French restaurant, but the Millars had been in France, and almost the first thing Margaret said (of course in ignorance of my table booking) was that French food had upset her stomach, and she'd had quite enough of it. Abandoning the French restaurant, I took them to my favorite pub, the Salisbury in St. Martin's Lane. There, settled on the red plush, I diverted Margaret from the idea that she could order a cup of tea. She settled for cider, but what was she to eat? Looking around with great interest at the people around us and the food being handed over the bar counter, she asked suddenly: "Is it shepherd's pie I see over there? *That's* what I'd like." The shepherd's pie was pronounced the best food she'd had since leaving the States, and on a trip they took afterwards they asked for it whenever they stopped at a pub for lunch. We ended a successful afternoon by walking round various bits of the West End, during which Margaret tried on and rejected several pairs of boots. She was very much a visitor to a strange country, Ken sweetly protective of her.

The radio program revealed a side of him I hadn't seen before. It was about crime and psychology, and included two or three interviews, including the one with Ken, which took place in his hotel. He talked with characteristic gentle candor about the background of his own books, and their quality for him as an attempt to come to terms with his own childhod. The producer Robin Brightwell intervened once, twice, three times, suggesting questions of a more direct kind that he thought I might put. At length Ken broke off and, without raising his voice or showing any sign of annoyance, said—I am giving the gist of what was said, not exact words—"Mr. Brightwell, I understood I was being interviewed by Mr. Symons. I should have been told in advance if I was to be interviewed by you, and perhaps I might not have agreed to it." It was one of the most effective put-downs I have heard, the more so because of its perfect politeness. When the program was transmitted I sent him a copy, and he expressed astonishment at the way Brightwell and I had put it together. "The level of civility was high, though I fear I didn't contribute to that aspect." He was surprised and amused to be paid a small fee for taking part, and gave the morsel of money to charity.

In conversation Ken was so withdrawn a person that it was hard to know what experiences were important to him, and what touched him only superficially, but it was plain from his letters that the visit to England lingered in his mind. He felt strongly the contrast between the crowded life of London and the "immense slow calm" of the Millars' life in Santa Barbara, recalled nostalgically the London Library, "full of peace and light," and of course lunch at the Salisbury. "So vivid were our recollections of that great pub in St. Martin's Lane that the first thing Margaret made when she got home was shepherd's pie." He was a little surprised to have attracted so much attention from newspaper interviewers, and particularly pleased that in the *Sunday Times* Philip Oakes had mentioned his "tip of the hat" to Auden, "without whose cheerful encouragement I might never have made it into print." A little later, reading a book of mine about the thirties, he remembered—something he never talked about to me—"the London of my youth when I took part in the anti-Fascist demonstrations and was chased by policemen on horseback." He went on to other things never expressed verbally:

I value the book above all as an expression of my dear friend Julian, for I know how much you were a man of the thirties—a desperate time when it was after all, at least in the democracies, remarkably good to be alive. I'm a man of the thirties, too, and if I hadn't been a Canadian I might have stayed in London and had a quite different life. But I had other fields to plough.

He returned to the theme in later letters: "I was tempted to stay there and go to the University where I had friends. But a Canadian-American with an education in English has to be careful in his choices. In the thirties, at least, it was regressive for a Canadian to go English, or so it seemed to me. That's probably no longer true. Canadians are finding themselves in Canada *via* England. But I was pulled back and processed through the giant American route, ending as that combination of qualities, a Californian, or perhaps just a Canadian after all." And again, years later: "If I had London available, I'd find it hard to stay out of it, and possibly even harder to live in it." He consoled himself with the thought that Santa Barbara was about the same size as Periclean Athens. "We live almost in the country, in effect, but five minutes from a shopping center. That doesn't *sound* too much like Athens, does it?"

Reading Edmund Wilson's *Upstate* he pondered on the possibility of writing something of the same kind. "As I get older and look forward and back, I wonder if I can undertake the kind of family and personal history that I could, and probably should, write. . . . It's too soon yet, though, to embrace all that old sadness, the substance of my mother, the shadow of my father." The outline of such a book can be glimpsed in some of the pieces collected together by Ralph Sipper and titled *Self-Portait,* but it is no more than an outline. The inwardness of those youthful feelings was expressed only at one remove, in the novels.

Our correspondence, not constant but without many breaks in it, dealt very little with crime stories. It marked the wide range of Ken's reading, from a new life of Ibsen to Gogol to John Berryman's last poems. He valued poetry above prose, and noted wistfully that "we prose writers secretly write for the poets and secretly yearn to be noticed by you." Reading the transcript of a discussion about his work that I did with Al Alvarez (I committed another gaffe by suggesting that he might not know of Alvarez, and was told that Ken had *The Savage God* on his shelves, and was a charter subscriber to the *New York Review of Books* for which at that time Alvarez often wrote), he said that he felt as if he had been buried in Westminster Abbey, then moved from joke to seriousness. "Actually I plan to have my ashes scattered in the Santa Barbara Channel where, in the destructive element immersed, I have spent the best hours of my best days." By this time he was famous in his own country, but praise from British literati seemed to hold special importance for him.

There is little more to say that wouldn't be repetitious. In 1974 I suggested that Lew Archer might have fulfilled his catalytic function, and that Ken would perhaps feel freer in his absence, and was told: "That is precisely what I am working towards—just between you and me," and that although "Archer hasn't hampered me much it's time I essayed something new, with the option of returning to him later." There was little sign, however, that his last book, *The Blue Hammer* of 1976, might have been the final Archer novel. In that year Kathleen and I visited Santa Barbara, and were greeted as warmly as ever. Ken had discovered the likely time of our arrival and suddenly appeared outside our motel, we had lunch at their splendid beach club, followed by an afternoon of swimming and talk.

We next met at the world crime writers' conference of 1978 in New York, where Ken made a speech, the early part of which was uttered rather as though he were talking to himself, with no audience in mind. The effect was odd, but seemed attributable to his public shyness. Later we agreed to meet for breakfast, and he came across from the Algonquin to where we stayed at its poor cousin the Royalton, a good hour earlier than we expected. Disturbing? We thought he had simply mistaken the time, but it seems likely now that these were advance warnings of his illness. Our last visit to Santa Barbara in 1981 was a sad one. When I telephoned and said we had arrived, there was a pause. Then Ken said: "Hello, Mr. Symons, I'll call Margaret to speak to you." At lunch the next day he smiled with his usual sweetness but said very little, and neither Kathleen nor I could be sure that he knew who we were.

One writes with regret at the failure to know better a man who was less withdrawn towards me than to most of the world. Expressing, on another occasion, regret for a failure to meet, he wrote: "I value your friendship above that of any transatlantic man, or cis-Atlantic either, for that matter. And the pull of Europe which I have kept narcotized since 1938, is beginning to stir again." The shelf of novels remains but, good as the best of them are, they are not quite what he hoped to write. It is a sadness that he will not write the autobiographical book about his youth that he contemplated for so long, or visit England again as he hoped and meant to do (the pull of Europe would never have taken him away permanently from Santa Barbara, but was still powerful), and that his writing life has been so abruptly terminated, with what might have been the finest things unachieved.

Paul Nelson

It's All One Case

It could have been for any number of reasons: maybe it was simply a matter of admiration and respect because the detective novels of Kenneth Millar (who wrote most of his books under the pen name Ross Macdonald) had touched and troubled me more deeply than almost any novels I'd read. Those stories of fractured families, reckless runaways and damaged young people who are haunted by eerie, early memories that *something* has happened—something terrible, but they aren't quite sure what—seemed both janglingly immediate and terrifyingly tribal, daring somehow to fiddle with the fuse of that timeless bomb within us all, planted somewhere in the past and set to go off who knows when.

Close to explosion in the winter of 1970, I had just finished the latest Ross Macdonald book in print. Perhaps that's why I committed an act of no small desperation and guilt: I reached out for at least the shadows of answers from the creator of private investigator Lew Archer, who, like Jean Renoir, knows that the real tragedy in life is that everyone has his reasons. My own existence was certainly a mystery in which the psychic murders seemed to keep piling up. I guess I felt like somebody in one of Millar's novels—those books to which, with hope, I clung—and badly needed a share of the understanding and compassion he'd shown his characters. For whatever reason, I picked up the phone one night, got his number from Santa Barbara information and called him. We talked of many things—none of them so dramatic as life stories then—and the connection was made. Later, we met, and I spent much of the summer of 1976 with him and his wife, mystery writer Margaret Millar.

Of course, in more general terms, the connection between Kenneth Millar—who died of Alzheimer's disease last month in Santa Barbara—and his hundreds of thousands of readers was always there: i.e., we all have families, and in all families, "crimes" are committed. Millar chose to write detective novels, and it was his particular genius to transform these familial "crimes" into murders, the staple of his genre. But "crimes" within a family are so psychologically complex and usually move in such wide generational cycles—think of your parents, their parents, your children, add (or subtract) some literal bloodshed and you have a case for Lew Archer—that attempting to solve them can be the most dangerous, albeit most important, occupation of all, one that surely requires a humane heart, an open mind, an iron will, and gloves of asbestos.

"*Solve* is the wrong word. Let's say *understand*," Millar told me when I asked him about the ramifications of his detective's repeated assertion, "It's all one case." Before that, the novelist had said: "The major plots and subplots are all related to one another, and you can't solve the main case without solving the others. This reflects my feeling that we're all members of a single body to degrees that we have no idea, except in moments of what might be called revelation. I think it's literally true—we live or die together. And the influences of just one person on another are absolutely staggering, if you trace them. It's the essence of our lives, that interrelationship."

For Ken Millar to understand and come to terms with his own life was a task nearly as formidable as any he set for his characters. Born in Los Gatos, California, on December 13, 1915, he was soon denied both his native country and his parents. His mother, a partial invalid, and his father, a sea captain-poet-journalist, separated, and Millar spent most of his youth living with one relative after another throughout Canada. "I counted the rooms I had lived in during my first sixteen years," he's written, "and got a total of fifty." In one of our talks in 1976, Millar said: "People don't attach the same importance to a fatherless boy that they do to one with a father. Their judgments of children depend a great deal on the children's immediate background. In those days, I was my father's son. If I were to turn out well, that would have been a miracle."

In 1938, Kenneth Millar married Margaret Sturm, whom he'd met years earlier in high school. They wed on June 2nd, a date that Millar would commemorate by making it Lew Archer's birthday. Millar received a doctorate in English literature at the University of Michigan, taught school and, following his wife's lead, began writing. In 1939, the couple's only child, Linda, was born. Ken Millar had a family again.

And in 1946, "it was sheer fate," he told me with a laugh, that returned him to his homeland to stay. "Fate, of course, operates through all kinds of instrumentalities," he added. "For example, serving in the Navy during the war brought me to California, and the movie industry brought my wife to California. She was on a train back to Canada when she looked out the window, saw Santa Barbara, fell in love with it, got off at the next station and went back. There you have a wave of causality. But the basic fact—now we're making a plot out of this—is that I was born in California and always wanted to come back."

The rest of the story should have been a happy one, and much of it was. Husband and wife kept writing and were active conservationists. But Millar's past refused to stay buried. Though he had consciously used Archer as a shield, "like protective lead, between me and the radioactive material," this method didn't always work. In his introduciton to *Archer at Large,* Millar wrote: "Ten years and ten novels later [in the mid-Fifties], seismic disturbances occurred in my life. My half-suppressed Canadian years, my whole childhood and youth, rose like a corpse from the bottom of the sea to confront me." Psychotherapy helped, and with 1958's *The Doomsters,* 1959's *The Galton Case* (a semiautobiographical prince-and-the-pauper tale about a young man returning to California from Canada) and many of the books that followed, Kenneth Millar took his place with Dashiell Hammett and Raymond Chandler as a master of the modern detective novel.

Death always has the last word, however. In 1970, at the age of thirty-one, Linda died of a cerebral accident. In 1973, Millar published *Sleeping Beauty,* a novel about a young girl who's disappeared. Lew Archer finds her and returns her to her family. The books ends like this: "Laurel lay asleep on the bed, a pillow under her dark head and an afghan over her. There was a telephone on the bedside table. Before I used it, I bent over Laurel and touched her warm forehead with my mouth. I could hardly believe that she was alive. . . . She stirred and half awakened, as if my concern for her had reached down palpably into her sleeping mind. She was alive. I picked up the phone and started to make the necessary calls." That's the kind of man Ken Millar was.

I remember so many things about him—his compassion, his intellect, his quietness, his sense of humor, his great modesty, his very great inner strength—but one particular vignette stands out. Millar is standing, hands in his pockets, on one of the rails at the train station where his wife first saw Santa Barbara. He's talking to his young grandson, Jimmie Pagnusat, about "flattening pennies as a kid on this same railroad line, way up north, way past Seattle, in Canada." He looks up and down the tracks and then jumps, hands still in his pockets, gracefully from one rail to the other. He smiles at us. For some reason, I remember thinking: we come to his novels for comfort in the disaster of our lives, knowing that he and Archer have seen us—and worse than us—and will dispense mercy and kindness or, if they turn us over, at least understand.

John D. MacDonald

Namesake

I became acutely and uncomfortably aware of Kenneth Millar in 1949, but I didn't know that was his name until weeks later.

Dorothy and I and our very young son were living in Cuernavaca. I had been publishing magazine fiction for nearly three years. Lots of stories and novelettes, not only in a savage array of pulp magazines but also in *Bluebook, Cosmopolitan, Liberty, Story Magazine, Esquire* and others, some of them too small and too temporary to mention.

I had not yet written a full length novel and had it published. That didn't happen until *The Brass Cupcake* came out in 1950. We were in Mexico where the living was cheap, trying to get enough money stashed away to feel more secure in my new chosen profession.

My parents were living in Utica, New York. So a letter from my mother went from 9 Beverly Place to 8 Jacarandas, saying, in effect, "What a wonderful surprise! Somebody saw your first book in Grant's Book Store and we read it and I liked it so much I bought a dozen copies and we've given them to all our friends, telling them you'll sign their copies when you come back home."

She didn't tell me the title, *The Moving Target,* because I had to know it, right?

I wrote a frantic letter to my agent, Max Wilkinson, in New York, asking him to please find out what the hell was going on. After I lived through a very rotten two weeks I got a detailed letter from Max. *The Moving Target* by John Macdonald (small d) was in fact by Kenneth Millar. Had I by any chance read *Blue City?* I had, and had liked it well enough. That came out under the fellow's real name, Kenneth Millar. He was doing these new books—this was the first of a series about a California detective named Lew Archer—under a pseudonym which he selected because his father's name was John Macdonald Millar.

Max went on to say that he had been discussing the problem with Mr. Millar's agent—I seem to remember it was Harold Ober—and the publisher and the agent were in agreement that everybody had goofed. They had failed to check the magazine index. In picking a pseudonym it is general practice to check the book index *and* the magazine index, because if you find a busy name appearing and reappearing in the magazine index, it is a good bet that it will be on a book one of these days.

Everyone agreed—I took this to mean Max, Mr. Ober, and Millar's publisher—that I could restrain them from using that name. I had that legal right. However, they suggested another way out of the dilemma. Mr. Millar was under contract to do a series of books. They had high hopes for those books. And it could be a very big handicap to have the second and subsequent books in the series come out under another name. What if they changed the name slowly? John R. Macdonald on the next one, then John Ross Macdonald, and then Ross Macdonald, with the idea that subsequent reprintings of the first three would be credited to Ross Macdonald.

I thought it over. By and large the writing trade is a class act. Every writer who has any sense knows that good writing helps everybody. And Max said in the letter he had read *The Moving Target* and it was a good piece of work. It is only the hanky-stompers who seek revenge for unintended slights.

I decided that it would be sensible to give my permission for Millar's people to go ahead on that basis. I repressed the urge to ask for reimbursement for my mother. I had but one caveat—that the Macdonald pseudonym would be used *only* for the Lew Archer stories. I felt pleased with myself for having been so amiable.

Five or six years passed. I'd had six books published and a lot more magazine stories. I was in New York City on one of my rare visits to that mecca of royalty rates. I had sold quite a few novelettes to *Cosmopolitan.* They had conducted a survey which indicated that when my name was on the cover, there was a measurable percentage increase in newsstand sales. And so I had established a pretty good rate with them—better than their average. Kenneth Millar had been doing well with the Lew Archer series, in hardback as well as paper.

I was looking at the magazines in a store when I saw a new *Cosmopolitan* with the legend on the cover, all in caps, A NEW MACDONALD NOVEL. I knew I hadn't sold them anything for half a year. I bought it and found out it was by Ross Macdonald. The use of capital letters on the cover blurb removed any big-D little-d distinction of course. I opened to the novelette and found out that it had nothing to do with Lew Archer. I got hold of a spy in the woodwork over at *Cosmopolitan* and found out that they had paid fifteen hundred dollars less than my going rate with them to acquire something they could put on the cover that would enhance the newsstand sales just as neatly as a story by me would have.

I couldn't get mad at the magazine because they were just out there doing their magazine thing. No holds barred.

But I remembered how *very nice* I had been about not exercising my right to restrain the use of my name. I remembered my single caveat. And the more I remembered, the madder I got. I finally went back to the hotel, phoned somebody and got Millar's address and sent him a virulent and intemperate telegram.

In due course I got a letter from him, handwritten on three sheets of yellow paper. It was just as intemperate as my wire, and the gist of it was that inasmuch as he was known and respected all over the world, who the hell was I to come along and tell him what he could and couldn't publish.

I finally realized on the third reading of his letter, that Kenneth Millar had never known a thing about my little caveat, that obviously nobody had ever told him. So he must have thought me some sort of madman.

I let it cool for a few weeks, and then I wrote a reasonable letter to him, giving him the whole history, and explaining why I had felt done wrong. It wasn't a warm and friendly letter, but it was reasonable. I even told him about my mother.

His response was cool but reasonable. He said he was sorry about the whole thing, that it was not his job to check magazine indexes, and it was not his fault his father was named John Macdonald Millar, and also, since he had never heard of my stipulation, and had not agreed to it, and would not have agreed to it in any case, he did not feel bound by it, then or in the future.

There would have been no point at all at that late date in trying to tell him that I could have enjoined him from using any form of the name. I let that letter cool too.

About a year later he wrote me about one of my books. I forget which one. He said he had liked it. I wrote him back and said I had been reading him all along and should have told him I liked his work too. I told him that it was inevitable that the readers were going to get us mixed up. Couldn't be helped. So we both shared one kind of good fortune—neither of us was disgracing the name.

Seven years ago while in Santa Barbara I went to a phone in a restaurant and called the number I had for him. All of a sudden, on about the third ring, I chickened out, hung up, and went back to the table. Reason: I don't like out-of-town strangers phoning me, and I assumed, reading between the lines of his work, that we very probably shared a lot of the same prejudices. And we had already said what there was to say.

Collin Wilcox

Free-lance Person

Publicly and privately, I have often acknowledged the debt I owe to Ken Millar. I first met him in 1969, shortly after the publication of my third book. My first two books, as the saying goes, disappeared without a ripple. The central character in my third book was Lieutenant Frank Hastings, around whose future exploits I hoped to build a series. Ken read the third book, and spontaneously wrote me an endorsement. Now, thirteen years and twelve titles later, the Lieutenant Hastings series is still selling throughout the world (modestly, but steadily).

Beyond doubt, I can thank Ken for some of that (monetary) success. To this day, his original endorsement is quoted on dust jackets throughout the world.

But the essence of my debt to Ken Millar has nothing to do with money. Over the years, he taught me what it means—really means—to be a writer. He never concerned himself with the obvious penalties and rewards: the publisher's checks (always unpredictable, usually smaller than expected), the reviews (good ones, bad ones, perplexing ones), the royalty statements (usually indecipherable). Instead, without fanfare or pretense, in simple declarative sentences that were always incredibly concise, he conveyed his credo: you decide what you want to write—*really* want to write—and then you write it. If a publisher buys it, fine. But marketability isn't the primary criterion. You must write your own book, in your own time, on your own terms. You hope, of course, that a publisher will take it. But if the book doesn't sell, it's not a defeat. Nothing is intrinsically lost. Indeed, rejection could be a rewarding exercise in artistic self-knowledge. And, besides, for a real writer—Ken Millar's kind of writer—a rejected book is always past history. If you're serious about your craft, you're already into another story.

For Ken, the term "free-lance writer" meant precisely what it says. It meant that you don't accept publishers' advances offered on a ten-page outline of a projected novel. To accept such an offer, Ken believed, made the writer little more than an employee, beholden to his publisher for approval—and for the last half of the advance, usually.

Ken learned, long ago, that before you can become a free-lance writer, you must first become a free-lance person. You must decide how you want to live your life, and you must then set about trying to work it out. You don't always win. But you never—*never*—quit trying. And you don't talk about it, you just do it. You listen to your critics, if they're sincere. But you never bend to them. Because you know that success—recognition for the ideas you've worked nto your fiction—is a very personal affair. It's something between you and your reader. It's what makes being a writer very important, and very valuable, and therefore very rare.

Over the years I have developed an all-purpose writers' conference speech. The speech's punch line may be a little fatuous. But it gets the essential message across. To the assembled aspirants I say, "I can tell you all how to succeed as novelists." I pause, watching interest quicken. Then, disingenuously, I add, "All that's required is that you never give up. You just keep trying."

For that homily, as well as for many, many other bits of wisdom too personal to repeat, I owe Ken Millar more than I could ever repay.

Michael Lewin

Afternoon by the Pool

I got brave in November of 1979. For the first time I wrote to a writer I much admired to ask if I could meet him. My dubious courage was rewarded. He wrote back to invite me to join him and his wife for lunch. I was as pleased as a private eye with a client. I saved the letter. I even saved the envelope.

While others contributing to this volume know Ken Millar better than I do or are better qualified to praise and place his work, it is probable that the careers of few have been as directly, if distantly, influenced by him as mine has. I even got the idea for my first detective novel while analyzing one of his. Having just read it, I grew curious about the degree to which the references and cross-references held up and were consistent. It was a reader's curiosity, but I was a writer so I went back through the book, page by page.

You won't be surprised to learn that I didn't find a single hole. The only possible question was whether a slightly pregnant woman mightn't be showing her condition by the time of the poolside home movies. A poor return for my sheets of chartings and chronologies.

Later, too, Ken's kind words written and spoken about my books encouraged both me and publishers at critical times. So, being on the West Coast for what might be the only time in a decade, I wanted to go to Santa Barbara to thank him.

I live in England. My trip to California in December was, apart from business purposes, to show off burgeoning kids to my mother, who lived then in L.A.

The invitation from Ken and Margaret included the children and on December 22nd the three of us arrived at the Millars' beach club in Santa Barbara around noon.

I'd been a little worried as I drove. Less about the children and their capacity at nine and ten for interrupting and distracting than with uncertainty about whether there would be anything to interrupt. I'm not the world's most sociable character and the potential for conversational off-shoots from "thanks" seemed limited.

But one is silly to worry. Especially if one is being brave. The Millars had been through this routine of worshippers arriving uncounted times. And the children scored big with the warm, strong, apparently robust Margaret and the lean and gentle Ken.

We talked easily and swam and had a real nice time.

Children provide a focus. Mine, the Millars' grandson Jimmy, and our own childhoods. Where had I grown up? What first memories? Ken remembers Vancouver and water and swimming a lot. My Elizabeth nerves herself gradually to lifetime first jumps off a springboard.

It is noted that in the long run it will be good for the children to have a double culture to draw on. How does my dual location affect my fantasy? More and more, I say, and I am about to set off on details of conceivable interest and significance only to me when a moment of lucidity throws up a mirror and I stifle myself, turn to the sea only a little way beyond the pool and ask, "Do you sail?" We talk of the island twenty-five miles across the channel, its future as a bird refuge, the sharks and currents which make the channel unswimmable.

In turn we swim in the pool. Non-swimmer-but-dog-paddler Roger does half a length, then a length, then two, then four. "Brave boy," Ken says. He shows Liz the Jacuzzis.

We come back and there are four wooden chairs and one garden type with cushions. Because it is patently too low for the table we will eat from, Ken defers to us by taking the cushioned chair. He sits. He sinks. "I sank lower than I expected," he says. "That's been the story of your life," Margaret notes, "sinking lower than you expected." "Also rising to unexpected heights," he says.

In the pool, Margaret has asked whether I'd met Ken before. I hadn't. When she introduced me to people at poolside as being "in the same profession as we are," I basked a little.

Above the pool the Millars speak briefly about a man they have seen in the club and explain that he is a friend who has just found out he has an inoperable brain cancer. It's the kind of thing that takes you off in a couple of months. He is downstairs "having a couple of drinks." They agree that it is probably the way to go about things in that situation.

Before long it is time for us to go.

I say my prepared piece to Ken about being pleased that he exists.

"You're not half so glad as I am about that," he says.

Is there anything specific I wanted to ask him?

Only whether it ever gets easier.

"No," he says.

And he offers an item of advice. Concentrate on the things coming into your psyche, not on the things receding, even if you don't like them.

Which seemed, even then, pretty good advice.

As we leave the club, I remember that there are presents from the children in the trunk (it *is* soon to be Christmas). Ken comes to the back of the car to take possession of a big snowflake from Roger and a sheet of vaguely cartooned jokes from "1000 Jokes For Kids" from Elizabeth. Ken is gracious and effusive and even seemingly touched by these unique items. Then he shakes hands again and jogs off in the direction of his car because we have made him late.

Noel Young

His Silent Smile

In the early fifties Kenneth Millar wasn't regarded by us as a particularly serious writer. We saw him more as a literary scholar who presided over our evening writing classes and conducted us on excursions through Faulkner country and the terrains of Flaubert, Dostoevsky and Fitzgerald. He read our efforts aloud in class and wrote painstaking commentaries sometimes longer than the work itself. He was deadly serious and showed impatience only for students who didn't commit themselves wholeheartedly to their work. Yet analytical as he was, we soon saw how he warmed up to the writers of feeling.

During his reign as our mentor he was usually stoic and confronted every level of student writing, from the gushings of a sentimentalist's journal to the strident voice of a young revolutionary, with equal aplomb. "Draw from your deepest and truest," he entreated. "Be willing to *work*. Tear your manuscript to shreds and rebuild it, dozens of times if necessary, until you have honed your language as best you can. Remember, you'll be living with your writing *for the rest of your life.*"

Ken's demeanor could be absolutely intimidating. I would never have dared, if I were within a lifetime of his presence, not to give writing my best shot. One night, at his urging, I brought a short manuscript to his house. When he opened his door and brought his dogs to heel, he beamed at me without uttering a word. I tried to chat and stammered an elaborate apology about why I was ten minutes late. Nothing I said could deflect his silent smile. Finally, when I'd run out of words and handed him my envelope, he invited me in. The silent smile reappeared. I backed off with the excuse of being late for somewhere else. As he closed the door I realized I'd lost a rare opportunity for an audience with a master. Fortunately, over the years to come, I encountered Ken many times again—at dinner gatherings, fund-raising picnics, writers' lunches, beach walks—and I came to learn that the silent smile was his way of listening to a friend.

His voice was deceptively flat and unequivocal. My first impression was of a scholar deeply lost in thought. Yet for all his intelligence and learning, he had sudden moments of passion when his voice would resonate (more a growl), and betray emotions far more sensual than you guessed he'd ever allow. Then you looked at him again, silent before you with his sloping shoulders, his firm torso, and you remembered he had been a college wrestler and still swam a couple of miles in the ocean every day, rain or shine. And it came to you then that the writers he dwelled on were hot-blooded ones, not intellectual reptiles.

We sat in his classroom, week after week for several years, during the time he was writing *Find A Victim* and *The Barbarous Coast,* without ever hearing more than the merest mention of his own work. He divulged practically nothing about himself and would rather read from *Winesburg, Ohio* or Eudora Welty's latest story. How were we to know that Ken's true calling wasn't teaching and that he only wrote what we thought were pot-boilers for bread and butter? Some years later, however, I chanced to read *The Galton Case* and got hooked. Millar, I suddenly realized, had turned crime writing into *literature.* I became a fan and read everything of his I could lay my hands on. About this time he gave up teaching and became recognized as Ross Macdonald, profound writer of hard-hitting drama, both the thinking man's crime writer and the street reader's intellectual. His books were equally at home in Greyhound buses and in university libraries.

Life can take strange turns. In the fifties I was his awed student, and in the eighties I found myself his awed publisher. *Self-Portrait,* his only collection of personal writings and the closest thing to an autobiography he was ever to do, became my unexpected privilege to publish. I was dumbfounded one day when Ralph Sipper called me to say Ken, a person who never tipped his hand, had given the book his blessings. As we began the project we litttle suspected this journey "ceaselessly into the past" would be his last book.

He was always a mentor to me, even after his teaching days. Some years ago when I underwent my stint as a bachelor, I encountered Ken in the checkout line of a small supermarket. It was Saturday afternoon, I felt desolate and must have let it show in my eyes. Although Ken hadn't seen me for several years and didn't know my status, his intuition came into play. He put a comradely hand on my shoulder, looked me squarely in the eye and said with some urgency, "Get someone to live with you. *Anyone.*" I took his advice and it saved me.

Ken's silent smile, once so intimidating, would comfort me now.

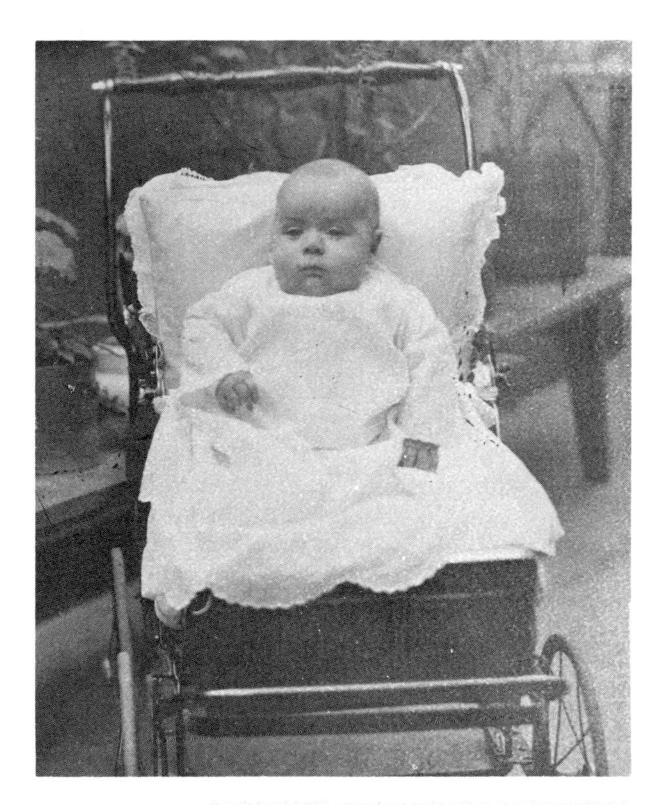

*Kenneth Millar,
age three months
and nine years.*

Kenneth Millar, circa 1940 at the Kitchener-Waterloo Collegiate Institute where he taught school.

Lt. (jg.) Kenneth Millar during World War II.

Kenneth and Margaret Millar in early Santa Barbara days.

With daughter Linda on the Santa Barbara strand.

Kenneth Millar (and friend) taking his daily swim in the Pacific Ocean.

A Santa Barbara response to the 1969 oil spill. The Millars are seated.

With Eudora Welty at the Millars' beach club.

The Millars in their Hope Ranch home.

The Millars with actor Peter Graves, who portrayed Lew Archer on television.

With the editor in 1976, signing copies of The Blue Hammer.

One of the last photographs of Kenneth Millar, taken in 1981.

Otto Penzler

On Publishing Ross Macdonald

It must surely be the dream of any publisher to have on his list an author who receives critical acclaim from every corner, someone so highly regarded that an unbroken string of huzzahs, from even the most demanding reviewers, follows every new volume.

Not far behind in publishers' dreams must be having an author who enjoys enormous popular success, whose books are snapped up by an enthusiastic public and sales attain heights resulting in a lovely warm rain of black ink.

The perfect dream, of course, is when a publisher enjoys an association with a Ross Macdonald, whose novels in the 1960s and 1970s leaped onto the best-seller lists while continuing to get the kind of critical appreciation accorded few novelists in the past half-century and almost no popular American writers of any era.

I founded The Mysterious Press in the fall of 1975. The use of the word "founded" is both vague and euphemistic. There was a grand plan. There was nothing else.

The concept was to help elevate mystery fiction to the level it deserved. For too many years this complex, demanding and, often, cultured literary genre had been relegated to second-class status, dismissed as "mere" entertainment, or "pure escapism," or "popular culture." It seemed appropriate to produce works of crime fiction with the same affection and respect accorded precious little volumes of poems, *belles lettres* and intense miscellaneous writings revered by bibliophiles interested in "serious" literature.

Since no publisher seemed able or willing to treat distinguished mystery writers with the same respect given to some minimally gifted poets and authors of allegedly loftier literary endeavors, I determined to do it myself.

Good writers of mystery fiction deserved handsome bindings, crisp white paper, and fancy collectors' editions. They, too, ought at last to have their works produced in well-designed and enduring format: books worthy of their art. Here was new ground to be broken in the world of mystery publishing!

Never mind that my knowledge of publishing was akin to my familiarity with black holes and my skill as a brain surgeon. Never mind that I figured if I produced a thousand books to sell at ten dollars a book, and if it cost five thousand dollars to make the books, I would make a reasonable profit of five thousand dollars. Never mind that I thought I would design my own books (after all, how hard could it be?) and get a printer through the yellow pages (and thought that typesetting was part of the printing process and handled by the same company). And never mind that I believed most mystery writers sold about a hundred thousand copies or so in hardcover and that all I needed to succeed in this business was to find one out of every hundred fans of a given author and wait for the checks to start pouring in.

It came as more than a small surprise to note that none of it quite worked that way. Still, after cajoling some investment money from friends and becoming acquainted with Dennis Grastorf (who became the designer, art director and production manager for the books published by The Mysterious Press), we began to release some good books with more realistic expectations.

It did not take long for me to want to publish my literary hero, Ross Macdonald. But what to do about it? Certainly it was hopeless to think of publishing a new novel. Alfred A. Knopf had published him nicely and successfully for many years, and there was no reason to think that Macdonald ever would (or should) take a book away from that house.

A little research revealed that the first piece of fiction Macdonald wrote was done while he was in high school. It was a parody of Sherlock Holmes called "The South Sea Soup Co." which had been published in his yearbook and never reprinted.

Written at the age of sixteen, it was a competent, if undistinguished, piece of humorous prose that would surely interest readers today. With a potential readership comprised of the fans of Holmes as well as those of Macdonald, it was the very thing. Perfect. I suggested a handsome little edition, something tastefully exciting to appeal to the thousands who would undoubtedly clamor for a copy. Did Mr. Millar share any of this enthusiasm, I wondered.

"No."

The response was more gracious than the monosyllable suggests. "From where I sit now," he wrote, "I don't like the idea of making any kind of fuss over 'The South Sea Soup Co.' It's a fairly routine imitation of Stephen Leacock parodying Holmes, and shows no particular promise. I'm afraid it would simply make me look silly."

But there was an alternative, and it was gently offered. From about 1956 onward for several years, Millar had reviewed serious fiction and non-fiction for the book pages of the *San Francisco Chronicle.* If I thought the material worth collecting, he would be willing to have The Mysterious Press publish it.

An exchange of correspondence began with the *Chronicle,* ultimately revealing that it kept no records of what had been written by Millar. It did maintain a file of every paper that had ever been published and it would be possible to go through the microfilm copies of those years that were appropriate. Not unreasonably, the *Chronicle* was unwilling to perform this service, but it had no objection to my doing it. While contemplating the possibility, chance brought me to California and, happily, to Santa Barbara for lunch with Kenneth and Margaret Millar.

Hours were spent in the warm sun at their cabana on the beach, Ken and I eating, drinking and talking while Margaret scurried in and out, back and forth, attending to seemingly endless chores.

It would be stretching the point to say that it was perfect. I was nervous, afraid of making a fool of myself, fearful of being gushy; I had even brought along some first editions to be inscribed. And Ken, however charming he was, was not an easy conversationalist. As a relative stranger to him (we had not met before, our only contact having been an occasional telephone call and some letters) it was agonizingly evident that he was more than a little shy and no good at all at making inane small talk. Nor am I. Little flurries of question-and-answer, or vapid remarks about the weather or the food or the beach, punctuated long silences. They may have lasted ten seconds or so, but at the time they felt like jail sentences. What now? Do I remain quiet and give the man a moment of peace in which to eat his chicken? Then the silent tension builds as he thinks—

as he *must* think—that I am a colossal dullard and a bore of superhuman magnitude, with nothing of even moderate interest to say. Or do I ask still another question—one which he must surely have answered a thousand times, nay, *ten* thousand times, in his life—making our afternoon conversation assume the general tone of an interrogation?

Somehow, incredibly, the talk turned to the book he had suggested and which I wanted to publish. We discussed possibilities ranging from selecting a variety of his essays and reviews from all sources to making the book comprehensive, to include every published line he'd ever written in a critical capacity.

An idle remark changed everything. I don't know whether it was caused by tension, or a bit too much of the cool white wine, or too much California sun, but I finally blurted out that, while the book under discussion would certainly make a fine volume, it wasn't the ultimate book. It wasn't . . .. well, it wasn't the *dream.*

"What," he quietly asked, "is the dream?"

"To collect all the Lew Archer short stories in a single volume."

"Fine. Go ahead."

It could not be true, but it was. I felt like a thief who had planned the heist of the crown jewels and somehow had them in my hands. The first impulse was to put them back.

"Why," I asked, "would you let me publish the book rather than your regular publisher?"

"They never asked."

So there it was. I returned home and got to work. Bantam had published a collection of some of the Lew Archer stories in 1956 but there had never been a complete collection nor had there been a hardcover edition in the United States.

Arrangements were made with Millar's agent, clearance was obtained from Knopf, copies of all the stories were located. All that was needed before going to press with the book was an introduction from the author. The stories covered a wide range of years and, I felt, it was necessary to have some words from their author to put them into historical and creative perspective.

"No."

Once again, a negative response, and again couched in the most gracious, if emphatic, language.

In declining to write an introduction, Millar explained that it "would not only be difficult for me, but self-defeating. The basic story of the books is Archer's life, past and present. For me to write a revealing piece about him would foreclose further development in the books and use up too much of my subject. I'm afraid I simply can't do it."

That may have seemed like a negative response to some. I simply regarded it as the beginning of a conversation. In the end the introduction arrived. It had no form that could have been expected or predicted, mentioning Archer only briefly, but it is a splendid essay on the role of the private detective in society and literature. Like the novels, it reveals a great deal about Archer, and his creator, but quite indirectly.

When, at last, *Lew Archer, Private Investigator* (nine stories *with* an introduction) came back from the typesetter and was proofread, the print order went in. As with the four books previously published by The Mysterious Press, the first printing was to be 1,000 copies of a regular trade edition, plus a special collectors' edition of 250 copies, each numbered and signed by the author, with a slipcase.

Knowing this was a special book, I produced a promotional pamphlet, announcing the book and printing Millar's introductory essay. It was mailed to book reviewers, other members of the press who might use it to promote the book, some of the bigger bookshops and wholesalers, and individuals who might be persuaded to buy a copy of the book.

It worked. *The New York Times* decided to publish the entire essay in its Sunday Book Review section, in which the book was also reviewed favorably and at length. Advance orders arrived in numbers that I had never before experienced.

Before the first printing was off the press, we ordered a second printing, this time of 2,000 copies. The Detective Book Club took it as a premium and as a selection—the first time that either of the major mystery book clubs offered a book by a small press. Within three months, we had ordered a third printing and then a fourth. Six thousand copies of *Lew Archer, Private Investigator* are in print. A modest number, perhaps, but astonishing when one recalls that there were no salesmen, no advertisements, no distributors to help sell the book. All copies are sold via mail order—addressed to a post office box and filled as I typed labels and invoices in my Bronx apartment while my brother packed and shipped one carload after another. Could an author have a greater tribute than seeing his fans take such pains to track down his new book and buy it?

It is not important that I had so much affection for the book that I spent too much to produce it, insuring that—no matter how many copies sold—it would never really turn a profit.

What is important, and transcends every other aspect of that joyous product, is the relationship that developed from it, the friendship that reduced the geographic distance between Ken and me.

Our contact revealed to me an aspect of Ken Millar's personality which is, if not downright unique, extraordinary and admirable: a type of humility mixed with pride that I have never recognized in another human being.

Nothing is more memorable about my conversations and correspondence with Ken Millar than his genuine sense of being surprised, grateful and flattered that someone was interested in his work, or approved of it, or even cared about it. There can be no doubt that Ken felt good about his work, that he was proud of it, and that he knew that a lot of people shared his affection for it. He knew what he wanted to do with his art, he worked hard to accomplish it, and he was gladdened by the result.

Still, I always had the feeling (and it was nothing more concrete than that) that he thought it might somehow disappear, that Lew Archer might be forgotten, that his books would no longer be read, that his place in the history of American letters was tenuous.

If I have understood him in this, it is the only time that Kenneth Millar's judgment has been flawed.

Jerry Speir

Writing Ross Macdonald

I should have known better.

I was rapidly approaching the deadline on the book that I had been commissioned to write on Millar's novels. I had postponed trying to persuade him to a telephone interview until I felt confidence in my own command of his work. Unfortunately, neither I nor my publisher could afford to fly me to the coast to do things properly, in person.

I had been warned that he was not particularly fond of interviews. My first letter to him ran to six pages, single-spaced, which, after a brief statement of who I was and what I was up to, proceeded to endless questions of tedious detail regarding his intentions in specific novels.

His reply came on less than one full sheet of typing paper (torn neatly across one end as if with a ruler) covered in his inimitable, tiny hand. "I have no taste for working with you on your projected book to the extent that your long and detailed letter seems to suggest," he wrote. "You can assume that just about everything in my books is intended. . . . Bear in mind that I don't re-read my own books and have only the fuzziest memory of most of them. Nor do I intend to study them and re-read them now."

It was not a total rebuke. He did agree to talk with me on the telephone, after all. And what had I expected anyway? Perhaps I had assumed that, given my fancy display of erudition regarding his work, he would be inspired to a spontaneous overflow of biographical anecdote and literary insight that would have provided me with what news types call a "scoop." I had much to learn. Despite his novels' emphasis on the backgrounds and histories of characters, Kenneth Millar, I was to discover, did not dwell in the past.

And so, when the appointed time rolled around for our interview, I was more than a little anxious. What *would* he want to talk about? What *were* the right questions? With his approval, I had rigged an amateurish set-up for taping our conversation. Quite early on, it was obvious that the machinery was not working. My anxiety surged. Now I was reduced to frantic scribbling. His Scottish-Canadian accent, which I had not anticipated, gave the event an exotic air. And the pauses in his answers led me to jump in with still more questions before he had actually finished. At one point, he admonished me for the practice, arguing that his mind worked in slow, methodical rhythms and begging my understanding.

The telephone, though a marvelous instrument, is surely less than perfect for interviews. Still, we persevered and got through it, Millar virtually leading me by the hand. His memory, I quickly recognized, was far from "fuzzy," as he had claimed, on the particulars of individual novels. But it was not individual novels he wanted to talk about. What engaged him was the writer's process and the writer's desire to communicate and, yes, to educate.

When I persisted in asking specific, inane questions, like whether, in his Navy days, he ever actually experienced a fire aboard ship like the one that figures in *Sleeping Beauty*, he was patient. Not really, he said. There had been a "similar occurrence," but what was important was the writer's ability to "take the force of an event and mask it but preserve the emotional and psychological power." It is a simple statement, as I reflect on it now, but one which I have reconsidered many times as I have worked at my own fiction, or when I have heard others say something like "Boy, I could write a great book, but I'd be sued." Most people who operate in the real world with their eyes and ears open encounter enough material for a novel in the average week. But only the talented and the dedicated can *transform* that material into a fiction that preserves the emotional and psychological power of the original without the sources being identifiable—or even relevant. Fiction, I took Millar to say, is the art of transforming the personal and specific into the common and universal.

In answer to another question, which tried to pin him down on the "message" of his books, he explained that he didn't write "with the thought of putting in specific ideas," but rather—and obviously—

the ideas which did find their way into his novels were simply a product of his life and observations, of a certain "psychological causality." "Whatever I did," he said, "came naturally."

What "came naturally" to Millar with his wide-ranging, unique background began, of course, with his first-hand experience of a disjointed family in a disjointed modern world. The difficulties of those times launched him on a personal search for identity and continuity that is repeatedly reflected in his novels and that benefits from the double perspective of his "dual nationality." He also "came naturally" to the class and social consciousness that grew partly out of his stint as a farm laborer during the Depression and to his sense of the global change in the "emotional and spiritual tone" of the "moral landscape" fostered by war and reinforced by his own sojourn in World War II. Intellectually, his interests in psychology no doubt developed out of a sharp self-consciousness and blossomed "naturally" in his dissertation on Coleridge's psychological criticism—just as his literary interests "naturally" grew to include the likes of Proust and Dostoevsky, of Anne Radcliffe and Raymond Chandler. Closing the physical circle of his life with his move back to California after the war, it is only "natural," perhaps, that California should become the center of his personal mythology and that its oil spills and raging brush fires should figure prominently in his critique of our rapacious, alienated age. And it is only "natural," no doubt, that all these experiences have contributed to his concern for the relationship between the individual and a "technology [that] is sweeping away all meaningful relationships," to his depiction of the search for value in the modern world, and to his chronicling of the evil inherent in unconscious egoism.

Still, I could not be satisfied at the time with the explanation that it all simply "came naturally." When I tried to press him further on his specific ideas and intentions, he again generalized. "It is the purpose of fiction," he said, "to take the most difficult and complex subjects into a light where they can be grappled with. It is up to writers to understand and present conflicts so that the humanity of all sides is made clear."

When I went back to the novels, I realized that "making clear the humanity of all sides" could serve as a fair thematic summation of Millar's canon. Not only are we led to understand the humanity of Lew Archer—arguably the most human-sized, fallible, sympathetic hero in detective fiction—but we are also enlightened on the subject of the humanity of even such unlikely and unlikeable characters as Colonel Ferguson, a portrait of the wealthy victimized by wealth in *The Ferguson Affair,* or Alicia Hallman, the murderously alienated, witch-like mother figure in *The Doomsters.* Always we are given enough explanation to understand even the most bizarre actions of the most despicable characters. What we are offered is a window on the psyche of the time, an insight into how and why such characters exist. We are encouraged (by the pawnbroker Kaufman in *Blue City*) not to "simplify too much" and we are reminded (by Millar in a 1967 *New York Times* interview) that the psychological insights of Coleridge and others, which have been articulated for our century by Freud and all his disciples, have "deepened our moral vision and rendered it forever ambivalent." Seeking to find fault and place *blame* is then, as *The Wycherly Woman* emphasizes, a shallow and insufficient response to the world. "People should take a close look at themselves," Archer tells us in that novel. "Blaming is the opposite of doing that."

None of this should have been news to me. What I eventually realized was that, in my interview, I had made the same mistake as many of the critics I had been reading. I was asking Millar about the specifics, the "tricks," of constructing particular novels; he was answering me, on the other hand, in terms of "the purpose of fiction." Though he allowed that he was "not claiming the *highest* importance" for the detective genre, he did indicate that he saw it as a very useful vehicle for confronting the contending forces of our time and as an effective means "to reach people and educate them."

Millar best elaborated his thoughts on the merits of popular fiction in his interview with Jon Carroll for the June 1972 *Esquire.* That statement, which is still the best I've ever read on the subject, went like this:

> I have a very strong feeling that it's the duty of a writer, or at least this particular writer, to write popular fiction. Ideally a community tends to communicate with itself through its fiction, and this communication tends to break down if there are Mandarin novels written for Mandarins and lowbrow novels written for lowbrows, and so on. My aim from the beginning has been to write novels that can be read by all kinds of people.

That it is "the *duty* of a writer . . . to write *popular* fiction" is a notion which may well surprise some, especially certain Mandarin academics. But Millar's point, I think, is typically succinct. The novel is a field of mass communication; anything which limits its reach also limits its power and divides rather than unifies.

And Millar's intent, of course, is always to unify. Whether he is exploring the theme of alienation and the naiveté of the classic American hero, of the personal corruption and lack of love at the heart of a foundering society, or of universal guilt and the thread it weaves into the past, the effect of Millar's novels is almost invariably a sense of the positive possibilities of the human condition. Even though we may, at times, have suspected, along with the narrator of *Trouble Follows Me,* "that all of us were adrift on a starless night, singing in the dark, full of fears and laughing them off with laughter which didn't fool anyone," we sense that Millar remains an optimist. As he put it in our conversation, "It takes a certain amount of lift to handle heavy material." Despite the sadness and misery of stories like those in *The Blue Hammer* or *Black Money* or *The Zebra-Striped Hearse* or *The Galton Case,* there is that lift at the end provided by the restoration of families or the recognition on the part of a central character of his or her responsibility for the horrors of the past as well as their accountability to the future.

I still marvel at the construction of *The Doomsters* and the statement it makes on the theme of inescapable personal responsibility. Archer is the character who experiences that book's recognition, and that scene does much to humanize him as well as to expand on Millar's favorite theme. At the end of the story, Archer comes to realize "the day in the past when this story should have begun for me, but didn't." It was a day when he brushed off an acquaintance seeking his help. Had he offered the help, that offer might well have been all that was needed to derail the train of violent events that followed. "The current of guilt," he learns, "flowed in a closed circuit if you traced it far enough." Though the revelations of psychology may have rendered our moral vision "forever ambivalent" and, in so doing, made the process of fixing *blame* meaningless, still, Millar argues, we can never escape our personal responsibility for the way we deal with our fellow humans and the world. Self-awareness is the key to our survival as a species.

As an aspiring novelist myself, I feel I owe Millar a great debt for the lessons embodied in his novels and generously elaborated in our conversation and subsequent correspondence. Generosity, in fact, and genuine cordiality are the qualities which come most readily to mind when I contemplate describing Kenneth Millar. Dedication is another, dedication to "making fiction as true as it can be," as he told me, and to a certain "poetic intention." But the truth he seeks to portray is not one which we as readers of popular fiction are prepared to accept directly. Rather, much as Millar has spoken of Archer as the protective shield which allowed him to deal obliquely with the explosive materials of his own past, so Millar as mystery writer serves as detective hero for our society—allowing us an indirect means for re-valuing and revoking the stranglehold of a crippling past in favor of a saner, more human future. If such obliqueness is an attribute of poetry, then Millar's intentions are indeed poetic. And the fact that he has embodied those intentions in a popular medium of mass appeal makes him, I think, a writer of unique sensibilities and one worthy of our highest praise.

Donald Davie

On Hearing About Ross Macdonald

It is said that he laughs at himself,
Betrayed into such grotesque
Non-sequiturs. I am told he
Powerfully still plies his
Breast-stroke across the pool
That was the arena or focus
Of his most alarming fiction.

Focus, a pool; a fluid,
A watery hearth he found
For any of us, this
Californian-born and
Canadian-raised, this unfathered
Quester after arenas
Familial and stable.

The chlorinated hearth
He swims and swims has not
Held his mind together;
Keeping his head above
Private waters he
Absent-mindedly earned
A world-wide reputation.

Non-sequitur! No wonder
If, now his mind is gone,
He chuckles at the bizarre

Concatenation of
Circumstance that a private
Eye can disentangle
Retrospectively always.

Wonderful all the same, or
Wondrous, there in the thresh
Of the directionless lengths
Of days, how the artist snorted
And seal-like turned himself round
To plunge upon the next
Pitiless, pitiful fable.

Ken, you were a powerful
Swimmer always, tireless.
Not you tired, but your brain.
When you wrote *The Galton Case*
I fiddled with *Pan Tadéusz.*
(Sons sought fathers in both.)
Those days won't come again.

Reynolds Price

The Core: for Ross Macdonald

The mother did it.
All but endless skein of causes
(Crazed barbed-wire of any life
Longer than a week-old boy's)
Raveled or hacked to a nested core,
Discovers the final dread of dreams
(That new boy's dread since the spasm of juncture)—
Mother grinning, lovely, loyal as lapdogs,
Gore at her lip.

Diane Wakoski

George Washington and Lew Archer in the Desert

The sun on my tongue, like a fat-skinned August tomato.
The end of summer sunflower, hanging
its beast-head, heavy,
seat for Sleeping Beauty, smudged with oil spill,
Oh, California,
how I long for you, even your Doomsters, your Zebra-striped
hearses,
for your special Geography from Luna Bay
to Pacific Point, a world bigger
than the navel oranges that are
the first fruit, there,
the temptation of fuschia-hung gardens,
of foggy canyons winding down to the sea,
of spring hillsides of poppies, like wild goldfish scattering and
dipping,
of stucco houses and terra cotta roofs,
of driving, driving, all roads end in sagey, thymey quiet;
but this is my telegram
of congratulation
to Lew Archer, underground man, the poet of private eyes

CONGRATULATIONS. THE SOCIETY FOR WESTERN
FLOWERS AND DIANE WAKOSKI AWARD LEW ARCHER
THE *LYTHRUM SALICARIA* AUTHOR'S PRIZE

ACKNOWLEDGING HIS QUEST FOR TRUTH AND JUSTICE SINCE 1949. The *LYTHRUM SALICARIA* OR PURPLE LOOSESTRIFE IS A BEAUTIFUL WEED OF WET PLACES WHICH CREATES A SPECTACULAR SHOW OF ROADSIDE BLOOMS EACH SUMMER AND FALL. IN AWARDING THIS PRIZE WE RECOGNIZE THE COMBINATION OF POET AND PSYCHOLOGIST, OF ADVENTURER AND CRUSADER, OF COMMON MAN AND THE BEST INSTINCTS FOR TRUTH AND JUSTICE IN ALL OF US.

As usual I have been driving
all night,
cross country, a moving target,
now, in this fragrant desert night, sagebrush, yucca bells,
the dry piney scents of California-Nevada air,
blowing through the car. No
dalmatian driver with ivory grin,
only the passing lights of heavy semis, instant enemies
to those of us whose night vision is impaired,
the sparkling neon of Las Vegas pulsing like red and blue
hammers, tapping out

P O E T R Y

One letter at a time,
sometimes the name,

A R C H E R

flicking on and off,
reminding of another neoned gate
another entry, passageway,
George Washington's picture on the far side of the dollar,
currency,
black money or green, it is all a
gamble, Lew,
though you hate that American city so much.

Do you think
Las Vegas
is a destroyer of innocence?
or
the American family?

or
of the illusion that we cannot tell lies
or
that making a fortune can be
an honest
enterprise?
A R C H E R
A R C H E R
Same Spade's dead partner, Miles Archer,
(the way some people die/
so meaninglessly)
A R C H E R
the centaur, Sagittarian
bowsman
who aims for the heart,
investigator of Oedipal secrets;
Archer, I'll meet you here on the desert,
where George Washington, my father lives in retirement,
wearing the Marquis de Lafayette's shoe buckles.
In ceremony, we will present to you, one of the unique
Poets' Wild Flower Awards.
This is to say
we will read your books
as long as we read Whitman, Williams or Milton.
"This is just to say
...
they were delicious
so sweet
and so cold."

Cool thoughts on the desert,
in America's West.
You will not die the way some people die,
You represent California justice,
California poetry,
not just solving case after case, The Wycherly Woman's,
The Ferguson's
Affair, but also
the mystery of why Americans
sing,
sing,

for discovery
of the self. George, silent George,
will speak out here
on the desert, and Lew, you will not drop the case,
even when you are fired, you will unravel it,
then give the thread to Betsy Ross
who will weave us a new American flag, one
with another star that
represents Truth.
Poet and Private Eye,
single voices of the questing self.

David Madden

Tracing Out the Web

I know intuitively that Ross Macdonald is important in my life and fiction, but in ways I can't articulate clearly enough now to make this the personal tribute I would like it to be. For more than a decade before I read him, I had felt drawn to Macdonald for several kinds of reasons, none of them seriously literary, and I had wanted and intended to read his novels. For 15 years, purely literary reasons made me want to read William Gaddis's *The Recognitions;* reading it more than confirmed my intuitions. It comes to me now how oddly, in my private swarms of associations, Gaddis's vision and Macdonald's complement each other.

Some "serious" and "popular" writers (terms Macdonald himself readily uses) have always admired each other; each would like to combine with his own dominant vision key elements that have freer play in the other's. Macdonald has said of classic Gothic and contemporary crime fiction, for instance, that "they are a medium of communication between the popular and the serious, making the former more meaningful, the latter more lively." He appeals to me as one of the few writers who has struck a balance between serious intention and popular form. The private detective novel, he was convinced, could "spread out into a form of the general novel." The distinction Graham Greene used to make between his "entertainments" and his "novels" is useful. Macdonald successfully combines Greene's dual purposes.

When I was 13, writing far more than I read, still more attracted to movies than to books, it was superficial, nonliterary lures that made me want to read: Thomas Wolfe's photograph on the back of the Penguin edition of his short stories and James Joyce's picture on the back of *A Portrait of the Artist As a Young Man;* I was first drawn to *Mildred Pierce* by the movie but was turned away by the photo-portrait of James M. Cain that made him look like the junior high school principal who confiscated the stories I wrote in all my classes.

Even years later, after I had become an aesthete purist, it was Ross Macdonald's name (that I often confused with Philip and John D., and John Ross, which proved to be one of Ross Macdonald's variant names), his photograph, and the titles of his novels that attracted me. And I liked the sound of his real name. I was intrigued to discover that Kenneth Millar was married to Margaret Millar, whose *Beast in View* I had long admired. His literary insights impressed me when I read his *New York Times* front page review of *Cain X 3*. "The human figures in Cain's landscapes are in terribly rapid motion, most of it downhill, as in a vision of judgment." Eudora Welty's admiration of Macdonald himself in her *New York Times* front page review of *The Underground Man* struck me as odd but stayed in my mind as I listened to the praise of other serious writers and wondered what his appeal to them could be. The long PBS television program about him put a glow on my resolve to read him—someday. Such lures kept me circling around him and his universe, often just about to move into it.

I never had a standing interest in detective fiction, traditional or hard-boiled. The movie versions led me to Cain's novels. While writing a book about him, I felt I ought to read his contemporaries, but mainly other non-detective tough guy writers like Horace McCoy; the only Cain novel close to the private detective genre is one of his worst, *Jealous Woman*. But I also read Dashiell Hammett, Raymond Chandler, and many other private eye novelists, including the writer I thought would represent their successors, John D. MacDonald (only *The Damned*). In recent years, though, I had expected Ross Macdonald would prove in various ways to be the successor to the tough writers I most admired: Cain, McCoy, B. Traven, Dorothy Baker, Chandler. Cain was the only one of these I knew personally, and I was fond of him, but even before I read Macdonald, something about what little I knew of him appealed to me as if I knew him well.

As a way of forcing the issue, I accepted a request to write an essay review of *The Blue Hammer.* With no premonition that it would be his last novel, I was glad of the opportunity to realize my intention to read Macdonald. All the vague intimations as to why his work would excite me became lucid experiences, and I knew that eventually I would read all his novels.

But I didn't read another until Ralph Sipper invited me to write for this volume. Because the writing life Macdonald shared with his childhood sweetheart, Margaret Millar, had always stirred my imagination, I thought I would read their early novels and discuss their similarities and differences. I wondered whether a comparison of *Blue City* and *The Blue Hammer* or of his first novel, *The Dark Tunnel,* and his last might yield some insights. I read those, and then *The Galton Case,* inspired by his essay on the writing of it, and finally *The Underground Man,* which I had always expected to read first, and which I feel is the best of those five. I feel I have been there before—reading the Cain and Abel fable in *Genesis,* reading *Oedipus Rex, Hamlet, The Great Gatsby, Absalom, Absalom!,* and *All the King's Men.* The so-called imitator of Hammett, Chandler, and Cain transcends them; it is only Macdonald who has stimulated in vision and style *possibilities* for my own writing.

I now know why I had intuitively expected to like Macdonald as a person. Reading *Self-Portrait: Ceaselessly into the Past* recently, I was startled by the many general and specific parallels between Macdonald's life and work and my own. I like the man who never recovered from the loss of his father, whose childhood moves to 50 different rooms in many towns and cities left him disoriented, alienated, the man who "had learned the significance of borders," like a Graham Greene character, the man who credited movies with influencing his life and writing, the man who wrote his dissertation on Coleridge, who once said of his own fiction, "I do scholarship in the life of the present," the man who re-read *The Great Gatsby* every year, the man whose insights into the workings of popular art enhance my own interest in it, the man whose awareness of the importance of point of view and its relation to style I share, the man for whom imagery "is almost the essential element"—above all the man who could imagine and develop over three decades Lew Archer, who feels, imagines, thinks, and acts out many of his creator's own qualities.

Perhaps it is not apt to say "I never knew Kenneth Millar," for in ways truer than through actual friendship or acquaintanceship, I do indeed know him through the phantom circuit of the imagination, as the characters in Ross Macdonald's novels who never meet *know* each other through his inquiring private detective. If events in the creative process are the major events in a writer's life, one knows him most meaningfully through the works which that process produces. In discussing the writing of *The Galton Case,* Macdonald said, "Writing is an action as well as a passion." And "As a man writes his fiction, his fiction is writing him." In a 1973 interview, he told Sam Grogg, "Writing is a rarer form of life . . . my novels made me into a novelist."

Unable to focus my personal feelings, beyond what I have already said, I have decided to discuss in a general manner what I, as a writer, admire in Macdonald's psychological crime fables.

First, I want to declare that I also admire Macdonald's achievement for reasons that have nothing to do with my own life and work, because I have never and probably will never write a mystery, tough guy, or private eye novel (except for a tour de force called *Hair of the Dog,* about Frank Swaggerty, a fat private eye in my hometown Knoxville, Tennessee who in my private vision resembles Thomas Wolfe. This instant as I write, it comes to me with startling clarity that I have been groping through this parenthesis toward this light: Frank's search for 13-year-old Avis Satterfield ends in his discovery, on the verge of incest, that she is his daughter—a Lew Archer kind of quest that goes a step further than Macdonald, with his Oedipal preoccupations, ever went. Hearing that Georges Simenon writes most of his novels in 11 days, I wrote *Hair of the Dog* as a bravura stunt in 11 days in the summer of 1961, sixteen years before I finally followed the first, for me, of Macdonald's many mysteries of ancestry and progeny, *The Blue Hammer.* I realize now why that novel appealed to me so strongly—the compassion of the private eye as he investigates such mysteries is at the heart of *Hair of the Dog,* published as a serial in *Adam,* the blue collar *Playboy.* I'll step out of this parenthesis now) and write about Archer with a pertinence I had not anticipated.

In 1982, six years after *The Blue Hammer* made its impression on me, I'm inclined to suspect that Lew Archer had some influence on a sudden and dramatic turn in the development of *Sharpshooter,* an off-beat Civil War novel I am still working on. Without warning, in the writing of the 800 page first draft of the novel, the sharpshooter came alive in the tower of a mansion in Knoxville, Tennessee; the eye, mind, and voice of this minor character became a way of telling the separate but parallel stories of the two major characters. Macdonald calls Archer a man of action, but "his actions are largely directed to putting together the stories of other people's lives and discovering their significance. He is less a doer than a questioner, a consciousness in which the meanings of other lives emerge." Archer "is an eye. And an ear." The sharpshooter has evolved into the major character, one of whose traits is his compulsive fascination with the lives of the two men who were the major characters in the first draft. The sharpshooter is not certain whether he shot General Sanders or not, but he has the distinct feeling that, even though he was with General Longstreet in major battles, he missed the war somehow. So for 70 years, the sharpshooter is an Archer-like voice talking to himself and to others as he struggles, with facts, photographs, and imagination to piece together the fragments of his three years in the war; he discovers, as Archer often does, that he can do so only in the process of gathering into his own consciousness the lives of others.

Macdonald writes about his own life indirectly. Even when writing about a Panamanian boy who is not himself, "I'm writing out the shape of my life." He failed, as in early false start versions of *The Galton Case,* to write directly about his childhood. I have been able to write about my own childhood in several novels, but I have found, as Macdonald did, that the most expressive autobiographies are those that cast imagined characters into legendary or symbolic dimensions. "Fiction, when it is working well, lifts out of the writer's life patterns which tend toward the legendary." *The Galton Case* is "a story roughly shaped on my own early life, transformed and simplified into a kind of legend." It is in that sense that I call *Sharpshooter* my most autobiographical novel. Writing about Macdonald, I feel I am continuing to work on *Sharpshooter.*

"The underlying theme of many of my novels," says Macdonald, "is the migration of a mind from one place and culture to another." That is one description of *Sharpshooter.* Having read four more Macdonald novels this summer, I feel their lingering effect upon my various perspectives on the sharpshooter. "Contemporary life," says Macdonald, "is a moving target." For the sharpshooter, the Civil War of his past is a moving target that he strives to get in focus; I hope that what the reader sees will illuminate the present. Macdonald's statement that "detective fiction can remind us that we are all underground men making a brief transit from darkness to darkness" and that the underground man has "a sense of interdependence among men" poignantly describes the way I feel about the sharpshooter. Raised on a mountain, he is still an underground man, who develops a tower vision, a kind of omniscience.

Connections between a writer's work and his life always interested Macdonald. Connections between a writer's work and his *reader's* life may also prove interesting, perhaps vital, to the reader. To use Macdonald's phrase, "How, and possibly why may emerge in the telling."

The connection may even be retroactive. In 1970, Willie Morris asked me to investigate for *Harper's* the killing of an unarmed black soldier by Jesse Hill Ford, author of *The Liberation of Lord Byron Jones,* in Humboldt, Tennessee. In any situation that has something to do with investigating a mystery, of ancestry or murder, or both, I, like most literary Americans, think of myself as Philip Marlowe, speaking (with Bogart's voice) more than *doing.* But looking back, I like to feel that it was something in my manner reminiscent of Lew Archer's that moved key people who refused to talk with *The New York Times, Life,* and other reporters to follow an impulse to talk to me. Several times, I imagined that my efforts to trace lines into the past, into the earlier murder on which Ford had based his novel, put me in immediate peril; but I felt even more keenly that I had asked questions in ways that would lead back to me as Oedipus's did, that I had projected lines of inquiry, connection, and effect that would have positive and negative consequences 20 or more years later. In Robert Penn Warren's *All the King's Men,* Jack Burden, speaking of Cass Mastern, a relative of the Civil War era whose life he researches, says, "He learned that the world is like an enormous spider web and if you touch it, however lightly, at any point, the vibration ripples to the remotest perimeter and the drowsy spider feels the tingle and is drowsy no more but springs out to fling the gossamer coils about you who have touched the web and then inject the black, numbing poison under your hide. It does not matter whether or not you meant to brush the web of things . . . but what happens always happens and there is the spider, bearded black and with his great faceted eyes glittering like mirrors in the sun, or like God's eye, and the fangs dripping." Jack Burden is the reporter as detective whose search has far more personal effect than he had feared at the outset. He speaks in two voices: the meditative voice of a researcher into the historical past and the tough guy, Marlowe voice of a private investigator into what Macdonald calls "the archeology of the recent past." In Lew Archer, the two sides of Jack Burden are combined; Archer, of course, especially as he grows older, is a distinct creation, despite Chandler's charge that he is an imitation. I read Macdonald not to get Archer's solution to the crime at the end but to behold the web he has traced out.

Having listened to Archer through three of his tales, I feel that he, more than Marlowe, articulates the kinds of feelings and attitudes I had while tracking possibilities in the Ford case (I have not yet *knowingly* experienced any consequences from touching the web). I realized then that an investigator, like a writer, especially when one is both, talks to himself in an interior monologue a great deal, in a very clear voice. "Archer is a man of action as well as an observer and recorder," says Macdonald, "but the emphasis is not on his physical exploits. He is less the hero of the novel than its mind, an unwilling judge who is forced to see that a murderer can be his own chief victim."

I began by regretting that I was not yet able to talk about Macdonald's effect on me. Now that I am into the process, I worry that I am becoming *too* personally involved.

On the other hand, that Macdonald and his work shed light on a novel I wrote before I read him, influenced the novel I am now writing, and put into perspective my investigation of the Jesse Hill Ford case, about which I wrote 250 pages but did not publish, strikes me as far more than one can expect a writer to do to a reader.

As I read *The Blue Hammer,* I *did* begin to be aware of a quite personal reason for Macdonald's effect on me. Two mysteries, possibly related, surround the birth and death of my maternal grandfather, who died when I was three. As I delved into Macdonald's novels, I discovered, as many readers already had, his obsession in his life and work with Oedipal mysteries that reach far into the past. I took to heart what a pastor tells a young man in *The Underground Man:* "I think it is unwise for a son to attempt to delve too deeply into his father's life." About my grandpa's life, I feel "a growing sense of discrepancy," to use the phrase Macdonald applies to the private eye genre, "of something wrong which may lead to something worse." He says of the mysteries of the past, "Our own minds have secret places where the dangerous past still lies hidden," sometimes illuminated by "the guilty lightning" in the mind. I like his phrase in

The Three Roads: "The impossible future superimposed upon the ugly present in the presence of the regretted past." From each character, Archer collects a piece of a time-bomb; he is the fuse for the long-dormant explosion of the buried past in the dying present.

All my life, I have watched the psychological and spiritual effects of my grandfather's death upon his widow, his children, and his grandchildren. "Murder is an objective correlative," says Macdonald, "of spiritual death." The mystery of my grandfather's death is enhanced, as in an Archer tale, by the mystery of his parentage. With her illegitimate son, my great grandmother came down to Knoxville out of the Cumberland Mountains from a little town that straddles Tennessee and Kentucky. Nobody can tell me anything about her family, and only vague rumors about the father of my grandfather. My grandmother finally told me that my great grandmother may have been the servant of a wealthy family, and was paid to leave town, or that she may have worked for her uncle who was a farmer and that his son may have gotten her pregnant. In my thirties, I began to suspect that my incipient clawfoot deformity, corrected by surgery when I was 13, might be traced to that incest. When my son was born, the first thing I asked the nurse was whether his feet were normal. For the past two decades, I have been more preoccupied than ever with the question, Who was my great grandfather? My mother and I have driven into the mountains to search out possibilities.

Throughout most of my life, my grandmother and my mother taught me and my two brothers the romance that grandpa's enemy shot him as he washed his hands in the lumber yard where he was a nightwatchman. Using grandpa's old holster, my brothers and I used to play at tracking down his murderer. I vowed that when I grew up, I would indeed find the man and kill him. I was about 23 when my grandmother confessed that she had always believed he shot himself. I wrote a story about the effect of that revelation called "The Shadow Knows." My mother clings to the conviction (as did my two uncles) that grandpa was murdered to keep him from revealing an act of company theft by his enemy. (I have paused to make a note to myself to find out after all these years—I am 50 now—the identity of grandpa's enemy.)

Following Lew Archer's explorations, I have become even more obsessed with the need to solve the mystery of my grandfather's birth and death. The writing of this essay has been prolonged by a sinus infection and by sleepless nights as I tried to force the few known pieces of the puzzle to evoke the whole picture. Macdonald's novels dramatize the dangers and the questionable solaces of such a search, and his quasi-fictional searches will always be a part of my own quasi-actual searches. Looking back, I had to strain to trace minor connections and major parallels between Macdonald's life and work and my own; looking forward, I am convinced that the five times I have already listened to Macdonald's voice have made him a presence in my life and writing, and that the 19 other opportunities will in time have consequences I can not and need not now foresee.

Thomas Berger

The Justice of Ross Macdonald's Voice

On occasion I have lived in England, so as to listen to the language spoken as we ourselves cannot, and should not, speak it, and for a while I am refreshed to hear of house numbers that are "in" not "on" a street; events that take place in the wrong sequence, viz., "there and then"; phenomena that are different "to" not "from" others; and firms that perform plurally, as in: "Methuen are bringing out my latest in the autumn." It is in such subtle locutions, rather than the more conspicuous matters of vocabulary—"lorries," "lifts,' "estate agents," etc.—that one branch of the language is insidiously true to itself alone.

After a short residence in the United Kingdom I find myself conversing in a hybrid tongue somewhere between British and American, perhaps even, in weak moments, in the so-called Mid-Atlantic accent. While this can be an amusing exercise, my writing is inevitably affected, and given my frequent reliance on the homegrown American idiom, not for the better.

Resorting to one's fellow expatriates, who are in the same boat, is not the answer. Nor in fact is reading an American writer whose style is notably idiosyncratic. It seems to me that Faulkner would not relieve one's sense of disorientation—unless one were Southern, which I am not. But I *am* a Midwesterner, and yet Hemingway would be quite as unsuitable for this purpose as the man from Mississippi. If one must confine oneself to that generation, Fitzgerald would be the obvious choice (I was not amazed to learn, from Ross Macdonald's *Self-Portrait: Ceaselessly into the Past,* the valuable collection of pieces edited by Ralph Sipper, that *The Great Gatsby* was a favorite of the writer we are celebrating in the volume at hand and a novel which it was his practice, as it is mine, to reread almost every year).

But if one lived in Kensington in 1965, one might have walked down to the paperback bookshop midway along the west side of Gloucester Road and purchased a British edition of *The Moving Target,* as I did. Or was it rather *The Drowning Pool,* or *The Barbarous Coast,* or all three, or more? Whatever, I had immediately found the voice I needed, and I was captured for good. At any given time since, I have been able to boast that I have read all Ross Macdonalds in print—yes, including those also excellent works in which Lew Archer does not appear, such as *Three Roads* and *The Ferguson Affair.*

With reference to private-eye novels I mean it honorifically when I confess that the plots, book by book, soon escape my memory, after having sometimes eluded me on first reading—as I once had the brass to inform the Master himself, who had lately sent a characteristically overgenerous comment on my work to a shamelessly importunate publisher in search of jacket "quotes." But what I meant then and mean now is that I do not go to Ross Macdonald for puzzles, or the more vulgar sort of *frissons,* or to lay waste to an evening—though all of those pursuits are perfectly respectable, for my money, and I might well so engage myself with lesser practitioners.

I read Ross Macdonald for the purity of his American language, for his keenness of eye and precision of ear, for characters who show the "cynicism of a small-time thief," or speak the "legalese of a cell-block lawyer," or have not "much else to fall back on" but their vanity; for a female drunk who says, "I'm smasherooed"; for country courthouses in which reigns a "deep, nirvanic calm" and plainclothesmen with the "stubborn, thick-bodied presence of veteran cops"; and for chapters that begin:

> The ride to Quito, on an old bus sardined with weekenders, was long and slow and hot. A girl who exhaled beer fumes and mauve-scented perfume regaled me with stories of her bowling triumphs in the twenty-alley Waikiki Bowl on Figueroa Boulevard. At the Quito Junction I bade her a quick farewell and walked out to the pier.

In the last example, the peculiar Macdonald touch can be seen to advantage in "mauve-scented" and in "Waikiki Bowl," "Figueroa Boulevard," and perhaps most eloquently of all in "twenty-alley"! Only an artist can afford such elaboration of ostensibly insignificant detail;

a mere craftsman would not have the stomach, or the wit, for the extravagance. Yet it is no less admirable that having chosen his genre, Macdonald honors his responsibilities to the craft, and at any moment in his text such an apparently casual observation will eventually prove to be plangent—as in *The Zebra-Striped Hearse,* when a man's overcoat, with one button missing, first seen draped around the shoulders of a chilly, sullen girl-surfer at Malibu, is later revealed as a clue to a murder.

Ross Macdonald's work has consistently nourished me, at home and abroad. I have turned to it often to hear what I should like to call the justice of its voice and to be enlightened by its wisdom, delighted by its imagination, and, not incidentally, superbly entertained.

Jerome Charyn

Blue Eyes and the Barber King

I was drowning somewhere in the middle of 1973, lost in the muck of a new novel, some dinosaur of a book about a barber king and the republic of Andorra, when I discovered Ross Macdonald. I was sick of my own mythologizing and wanted something simple to read. A crime novel, why not? I happened to pick *The Galton Case* and it satisfied right from the start, with its lulling, neutral tone.

The book had a morphology I happened to admire—as if Ross Macdonald were in the habit of undressing bodies to find the skeleton underneath. Nothing was overwrought: landscape, language, and character all laid bare. But this was no simpleminded accident. It was Macdonald's particular craft, that "wild masonry of laying detail on detail to make a structure."

Wild masonry. That's what Macdonald's work was all about: sad, strange histories that crept between the tight, closed spaces. The lost son who surfaces out of a brutal, murderous past, and then is transformed into an impostor boy whose identity is born in the act of murder itself. And in the middle of all this searching is Macdonald's detective-narrator, Lew Archer, who is neither Marlowe nor Nick Charles, but a kind of deadly angel, the observer with genuine feelings who only invests a portion of himself in the text. Half of him is always elsewhere. Or, as Macdonald says: "Certainly my narrator Archer is not the main object of my interest, nor the character with whose fate I am most concerned. He is a deliberately narrowed version of the writing self, so narrow that when he turns sideways he almost disappears."

This narrowing lens allows Ross Macdonald to deliver both a landscape and a past without the least hint of sentimentality. Macdonald is able to murder while he lulls us through the book.

I returned to my dinosaur novel, *King Jude.* But things were still rotten in the republic of Andorra. I had nowhere to go with my barber king. I couldn't squeeze him into a narrative that made sense. Not wanting to abandon my barber king, I decided to scribble a crime novel and let Jude the barber boil inside my head. But I didn't have Ross Macdonald's lulling sense of line. My writing was scratchy, secretive as a snake. I couldn't undress bodies with my prose. And I didn't love California the way Macdonald did. I'd lived in California for three years. It held no mythic properties for me. I remembered rocks and redwood trees. I'd have to find my detective hero and bring him to New York.

I'd been a bodybuilder and a Ping Pong freak. My sense of the underworld came from pool halls and street gangs in the Bronx. I was something of an extortionist at twelve, but I outgrew that habit, and by fourteen I was studying French irregular verbs at the High School of Music and Art. What the hell could I write about crime? I'd have had to go to the library stacks and pull out dossiers on the most memorable thieves of Manhattan and the Bronx, but I didn't want a crime novel that stank of research. So I depended on my one bit of luck. I had a brother who was in homicide. I went out to the wilds of Brooklyn where he worked. I sat with Harvey Charyn in his station house near the beach. I saw the cages where all the bad guys were held. I visited the back room where cops would sleep after a midnight tour. I was Charyn's kid brother, the scribbler, and radio dispatchers flirted with me. I met a detective whose ear had been chewed off in a street fight, another who boasted of all the wives he had, a third who twitched with paranoia but was reliable in any combat zone.

My brother drove me to the Brooklyn morgue since I needed to look at dead bodies for my novel. The morgue attendant took me and Harvey around. All the dead men looked like Indians. Their skin had turned to bark. I distanced myself from the corpses, pretended I was touring some carnival with refrigerated shelves. It was Harvey who sucked Life Savers and seemed pale. I was only a stinking voyeur in the house of the dead.

But I had the beginning of a history of crime: the sad gleanings of a few Brooklyn homicide detectives. I traveled with them in their unmarked cars, listening to their hatred of the street. They weren't much like the warriors I'd imagined detectives to be: they were civil servants with a gun, obsessed about the day of their retirement. And because I'd grown up with my brother, remembered his muscle tee shirts, his longing to become Mr. America, Harvey seemed the saddest of them all. He's the one who read books at home, and I became the writer. He was the artist of the family, but I got into Music and Art and Harvey never did. I'd replaced my brother somehow, bumped him out of the way. I sat scribbling at a university and he had to stare at corpses. He told me about a renegade rabbi who lay rotting in his bathtub for a month, a fourteen-year-old pros who was trampled to death by a gang of pimps because she happened to labor in their territories, the victim of a gangland murder whose arms ended up in New Jersey while his legs were buried in a potato farm somewhere on Long Island. The guy's torso was never found.

I'd watch my brother's face when he told his stories. There was no ghoulish delight. He was delivering the simple facts of his life as a detective. I felt like the brutal one, feeding off his homicide lists. And so I began my novel about a blue-eyed detective, Manfred Coen. This Blue Eyes was an odd amalgam of Harvey and me, two brown-eyed boys. Coen was a Ping Pong freak, as I had been. And if he didn't have Harvey's coloring, he did have my brother's sad, gentle ways, a wanderer in Manhattan and the Bronx who dreamt of corpses, like Harvey did. I allowed Blue Eyes a mentor, Isaac Sidel, a honcho in the First Deputy Police Commissioner's office who grooms Coen and later gets him killed. Isaac was the sinister chief, and Coen was his blue-eyed angel, a kind of Billy Budd.

I scribbled a good part of *Blue Eyes* in Barcelona. I was thirty-six and I'd never been abroad. I'd landed in Madrid, wanting to devour every balcony on every street. I saw the Goyas in the basement of the Prado and felt as if my own life was being recast on enormous blood-dark canvases: the giant who devoured his children could have been born in the Bronx. I settled in Barcelona and wrote for six weeks.

I finished *Blue Eyes* in New York and carried it to my agent, Hy Cohen. He looked at the title page. "Who's Joseph da Silva?"

I'd decided to use a *nom de guerre* after having written seven novels as Jerome Charyn, and all seven sinking into invisibility. I'd invented a tribe of marrano pickpockets in *Blue Eyes* called the Guzmanns. Isaac Sidel is feuding with this tribe, and the Guzmanns become the agents of Manfred Coen's fall. Wanting my own sense of tribe, I'd picked a marrano name for myself, *Joseph da Silva,* hoping that his books might sell better than Jerome Charyn's.

But Hy Cohen convinced me to stay with Jerome. "Kid, you've had seven books. That's something of a feat. If you go with da Silva, you'll be starting all over again. A first novelist is a much more endangered animal than the author of seven books. They'll kill you out there."

So I published *Blue Eyes* without my *nom de guerre* and returned to *King Jude.* I scribbled on it in Paris, London, Edinburgh, Connecticut, and the Upper West Side of Manhattan. The novel thickened to a thousand pages, and I still couldn't find a home for my barber king. While I collected the pages, my mind seemed to be at work on another book. I was bothered by Blue Eyes' death and needed to revive him. So I started *Marilyn the Wild,* which brought Manfred Coen back to an earlier time of his life. Isaac Sidel had a daughter Marilyn, who keeps getting married and unmarried and is half in love with Coen. Isaac's ambivalence towards his blue-eyed angel was becoming clearer to me. The old chief resented Marilyn's attachment to Blue Eyes, though he keeps this to himself. He's a coward when it comes to his daughter and won't risk alienating Marilyn the Wild. We can smell the evil begin to build. Isaac is crazy about Marilyn, but she's much too independent for a deputy chief inspector. He can find no means of manipulating her, so he manipulated Coen. And by allowing Coen to get killed, he punishes Marilyn, Blue Eyes, and himself.

I still couldn't put Coen to rest. I had to write another book, one that continued after Coen's death. Isaac has become the chronicler of Coen. *The Education of Patrick Silver* is about Isaac's own self-affliction. Isaac has inherited a tapeworm from the Guzmanns, and it flares up as soon as Coen dies. He blunders through the city with that worm in him and dreams that Coen is still alive. Coen's death has taken him out of his neat little universe, hooks him with pain. Manfred and Marilyn were his only connection to feelings outside the police. They were Isaac's history. Now he has the worm.

I was hoping I'd finished the story. I had my barber king to dream about. But the Andorran novel stayed dead. It was invention that evolved without a personal myth. I performed magnificent pirouettes on the page. I danced from line to line and was left with boring decoration.

I went back to Isaac and devoted a book utterly to him: *Secret*

Isaac. It was the history of Isaac after his fall from grace. The sadder he becomes, the more successful he grows. The worm is eating him alive, but Isaac is now the Police Commissioner of New York. A peculiar thing happens. Isaac begins to cannibalize himself, to feed on his own worm. He's taken Blue Eyes' ghost inside himself. He becomes Coen and barks his own song of innocence and experience.

I thought of other books, a kind of Balzacian series of adventures, with Isaac moving about the country and devouring the United States. What city was a match for him and his tapeworm? But I haven't learned how to be Balzac yet. When I call my brother's precinct, the receptionist says, "Ah, you're Jerome. How's Blue Eyes today?"

I'm the celebrity of Brooklyn Homicide. Captains and lieutenants want me to write their stories. I'm their chronicler now. And Harvey? He begrudges the complications of the last three Isaac books. He prefers the purity of *Blue Eyes.* Manfred Coen came from the Bronx, like him and me. Manfred Coen went to Music and Art. I'm sure he remembers Coen as a weightlifter, but Coen was too busy being wooed by Marilyn to lift weights. Blue Eyes could have come right out of Harvey's precinct. Blue Eyes would have been one of the boys.

But I regard Manfred Coen in another way. Blue Eyes was a ghost long before he was killed. His mother and father were a pair of suicides, and Coen was the orphan from Music and Art who fell somewhere between Marilyn and Isaac and could never get up. His absence, dead and alive, seems to power the four books.

Isaac goes to Ireland in the fourth book, visits Leopold Bloom's house on Eccles Street. He's a police inspector who loves James Joyce, but his pilgrimage is more than literary debt. Isn't Bloom the father Isaac could have been? Isaac had manufactured his own Stephen Dedalus in Coen, but gave him perishable wings. He "makes" Coen, destroys him, and suffers the wounds of that destruction. And why is Blue Eyes drawn to Isaac in the first place? Is he seeking a permanent dad, one who won't abandon him? Or does he know that all dads are destroyers, the good ones and the bad?

What does an author know? For me, the four books comprise a vast confusion of fathers and sons. My own dad was a furrier who never spoke. He grunted some primitive language that was more like the call of a disappointed wolf. But I had Harvey to interpret that wolf's call. He led me out of whatever Bronx wilderness I happened to be in. He was father and older brother and a bit of a mum, though he abandoned me before I was twelve, beat me up in front of his latest girlfriend. He had his muscle tee shirts to worry about. He didn't need a skinny kid on his tail.

And so Isaac's worm had been sleeping in me a long time. It grew out of a rift between Harvey and myself, more than thirty years ago. Forget Brooklyn Homicide. You need Sherlock Holmes to uncover the roots of any fiction. I'd come to Harvey to gather material for an uncomplicated crime novel and ended up scribbling four books about him and me and a meticulous tapeworm.

I finally let go of my barber king. Andorra wasn't that magic place where boys and kings can heal themselves. I'd invented a thousand years of history for Jude, a chronology that was filled with wondrous details, but it was spun out of avoidance, a need to hide. *King Jude* is a cold book, mythology without a worm.

Perhaps I'd used more of Ross Macdonald than I'd allowed myself to admit. Macdonald rocks back into his past in *The Galton Case,* weaves a narrative around his own wound, a gnawing sense of illegitimacy. The impostor boy who pretends to be the lost son of Anthony Galton bears a resemblance to Macdonald himself, or, I should say, Kenneth Millar, since Ross Macdonald was Millar's *nom de guerre.* "My mind had been haunted for years by an imaginary boy whom I recognized as the darker side of my own remembered boyhood. By his sixteenth year he had lived in fifty houses and committed the sin of poverty in each of them. I couldn't think of him without anger and guilt."

Like any fiction writer, Macdonald is "a false claimant, a poorhouse graduate trying to lie his way into the castle." I'm another claimant, hoping to get into the castle with Isaac Sidel and Manfred Coen.

Matthew J. Bruccoli

Up from the Category Racks

Like Dashiell Hammett and Raymond Chandler, Kenneth Millar went from the paperback racks to *Dissertation Abstracts.* The marketing and packaging of his books reveal something about how the reputations of what publishers call category writers are made in the era of the mass-market paperback. For Millar the process was different from those for Hammett and Chandler. Hammett's work was completed before the paperback revolution commenced in 1939; Chandler wrote during the early paperback years. Both canonizations were largely posthumous developments. Millar's popular and critical reputations—which were symbiotic—peaked while he was still writing.

Kenneth Millar set out to write what he regarded as democratic fiction: novels that would satisfy his own standards while reaching a broad readership. He practiced a popular genre, and within the mystery he chose the characteristically American hard-boiled (not very hard-boiled in his case) private-eye sub-genre. He was fortunate in having all his novels published in cloth and doubly fortunate in enjoying the distinction that went with the Alfred A. Knopf imprint. Knopf had published Hammett and Chandler, as well as James M. Cain; and the imprint conferred respectability on a mystery writer. But populist writers find their basic audiences among paperback readers. (I bought my first Ross Macdonald in a bus station.) Many paperback readers never buy a clothbound book. Again, Millar was fortunate in having most of his novels appear in the Pocket Books and Bantam lines—which provided maximum rack exposure and a certain element of quality—rather than in the junk paperback lines which specialized in category fiction. The problem remained of moving his books off the racks. Not until seventeen years after the first Lew Archer novel did Ross Macdonald show a sales spurt, and that was the result of a movie tie-in edition.

Between 1944 and 1948 he published four apprentice Kenneth Millar novels: *The Dark Tunnel, Trouble Follows Me, Blue City, The Three Roads.* The first two were spy novels; the third was a hard-boiled treatment of municipal corruption that clearly showed Hammett's influence; and the fourth was a psychological suspense novel. Reprinted in paperback by Lion and Dell, these novels sold modestly. Lion tried to spice sales by retitling its editions: *The Dark Tunnel* became *I Die Slowly,* and *Trouble Follows Me* became *Night Train.*

Millar found his own voice at the same time that he found his narrator. *The Moving Target,* published in 1949 when he was thirty-three, was the first Lew Archer novel as well as the first to carry the Macdonald byline (John Macdonald in its first appearance). The Knopf edition received more respectful notice than mysteries usually attract, but the reviews were relegated to the skid-row of the mystery-and-suspense listings. Anthony Boucher, whose "Criminals at Large" column in *The New York Times Book Review* made him the most influential American mystery reviewer, announced: "Just at the time that the tough genre in fiction needs revitalizing, John Macdonald turns up." *The Moving Target* was not a commercial success. Knopf required one printing (probably less than 5,000 copies). The novel was selected by the Mystery Guild for a cheap cloth book-club edition; the Mystery Guild subsequently took nine more Macdonalds, but it did not provide the visibility or sales of the Book-of-the-Month Club or the Literary Guild. With *The Moving Target* Macdonald began to be reprinted by Pocket Books, which at that time dominated the market, but this novel required only one paperback printing.

Published in the same year as *I, the Jury,* Mickey Spillane's first novel, *The Moving Target* failed to establish Macdonald with the public, although Pocket Books tried to convey the impression that Archer was a very tough guy. The cover depicted two men fighting on a pier, with the caption: "The knife in my hand didn't stop him. He came at me like a bull!" Pocket Books was the paperback publisher for the next four Macdonalds (three of them Lew Archers), but complained that the novels weren't sufficiently crowd-pleasing—a defect that the art department attempted to remedy. On the cover of *The Way Some People Die* (1952), a bare-breasted female perches on a bed watching two men engaged in combat. The caption promised "Dope, delinquents and MURDER". Pocket retitled *The Ivory Grin* as *Marked for Murder* (1953), without consulting the author. The cover featured a blonde loading an automatic plus a female corpse and a flaming car.

Millar's pseudonym alterations confused the customers and impeded his recognition. With *The Drowning Pool* (1950) he became John Ross Macdonald, after John D. MacDonald complained about byline infringement; and with *The Barbarous Coast* (1956) he settled on Ross Macdonald. Nonetheless, many readers confused Macdonald with MacDonald. They still do.

Knopf tried to generate curiosity about their Macdonald by making a mystery of his identity. The dust jackets for *The Moving Target* and *The Drowning Pool* had a silhouette instead of the author's photograph, and *Meet Me at the Morgue* had an X-ray of his skull. In 1954 the Knopf dust jacket for *Find a Victim* announced: "Readers who have been puzzling over the identity of JOHN ROSS MACDONALD need puzzle no more. He is no other than Kenneth Millar. . . ."

The early Archers sold routinely in cloth and paper; only *The Way Some People Die* (1951) and *The Ivory Grin* (1962) required second Knopf printings, and no paperback seems to have gone into a second printing in the year of its publication until *Find a Victim* in 1955. Macdonald picked up an unlikely source of visibility in 1953 when *Cosmopolitan* printed the first of eight pre-publication condensations of his novels.

Millar was unhappy with Pocket Books, which urged him to put more action into his fiction; and Bantam became his paperback publisher with *Find a Victim*. Bantam's covers were more subdued than those provided by Pocket; but the captions remained exclamatory. "A smashing, new novel of vice, blackmail—and murder, murder, murder!" (*The Zebra-Striped Hearse*).

Up through *The Doomsters* (1958) Millar wrote private-eye novels that were clearly superior to the competition—such as it was. His fiction was distinguished by literate prose, a controlled point of view, intricate plotting, and the corrupt ambience of Southern California. But he had not yet found the Oedipal roots that would nourish his best work. In 1959, when Millar was forty-three, he published *The Galton Case* and commenced his probing of the ramifications of the past that became the defining characteristic of his subsequent work. Whereas the ad pages in the Knopf editions had heretofore made the mandatory comparisons with Hammett and Chandler, *The Galton Case* insisted on Ross Macdonald's own achievement:

> The "hardboiled" label which has often been applied to Macdonald's books does them a disservice: the fact is, they bear only a superficial resemblance to the standard hardboiled product. Critics use such words as "creative, subtle, compassionate, literate, meaningful," to describe them. Yet these words of praise are earned without sacrificing drive and bite, staccato pace, and some of the wickedest plotting ever perpetrated.
>
> . . . .
>
> For the first time Archer discovers love and hope at the heart of the human tragedy. We feel that this book achieves a new maturity. It speaks to people of all sorts, powerfully and imaginatively, about the basic hopes and dreads of life.

Nevertheless, sales for *The Galton Case* were unimpressive: two Knopf printings and one Bantam printing in 1960. The best Bantam could do with the cover copy was: "THE NAME IS LEW ARCHER. BY THE TIME I FINISHED THIS CASE I WAS LUCKY IT WASN'T PERMANENTLY ENGRAVED ON A STONE".

Ross Macdonald published a string of seven brilliant novels in the next nine years: *The Ferguson Affair* (1960—a non-Archer), *The Wycherly Woman* (1961), *The Zebra-Striped Hearse* (1962), *The Chill* (1964), *The Far Side of the Dollar* (1965), *Black Money* (1966), *The Instant Enemy* (1968). His work became more complexly plotted and emotionally stronger as he probed the causality of the past; but until 1966 he remained an underground master. Although *The Ferguson Affair* went into three Knopf and two Bantam printings—which prompted Millar to speculate on the advisability of abandoning Archer—none of the others sold well in cloth. *The Chill, The Far Side of the Dollar,* and *Black Money*—three of his best novels—did not require Knopf reprintings. In 1962 Bantam announced that their Macdonald paperbacks were "approaching the 2 million mark."

A sales acceleration resulted from the 1966 *Harper* movie, the successful adaptation of *The Moving Target.* (Archer's name was altered to Harper to accommodate Paul Newman's lucky-H superstition for the titles of his movies.) The movie not only sold a tie-in edition of *The Moving Target*—with the title changed to *Harper*—but also stimulated the market for the out-of-print Archers. Between 1966 and 1968 five Bantam reprints bore the slogan: "LEW ARCHER—THE HARDEST OF THE HARD-BOILED DICKS." At this point Bantam seemed to be promoting Archer as a hybrid of Mike Hammer and James Bond. The covers had photos of a handsome tough guy (presumably Archer) being fondled by a variety of lascivious women. By June 1966 Bantam claimed to have three million copies of Ross Macdonald in print. At this time Pocket Books republished *The Drowning Pool, The Way Some People Die, The Ivory Grin,* and *Meet Me at the Morgue.* Altogether there were at least sixteen paperback printings for Macdonald during 1966 and 1967. Nonetheless, paperback exposure did not boost the next novel; *The Instant Enemy* (1968) was not reprinted by Knopf. The size of the first cloth printing had no doubt been upped, but the audience for Ross Macdonald and Lew Archer was still primarily paperback mystery readers—many of whom apparently manifest little discrimination in what they read.

The breakthrough to both critical respectability and cloth best-seller status came with the 53-year-old author's twenty-first novel in 1969 when *The New York Times Book Review* accorded William Goldman's review of *The Goodbye Look* front-page treatment under the headline: "The Finest Detective Novel Ever Written by an American." (Goldman had written the screenplay for *Harper.*) *The Goodbye Look* was not superior to half a dozen of the earlier novels. But it was the one that lightning struck. Millar's time had come. As often happens, it came late. Thereafter both the cloth and paperback editions of Millar's novels proclaimed that they were "The Finest Series of Detective Novels Ever Written by an American." Knopf required eight printings of *The Goodbye Look,* and the novel was distributed by the Literary Guild. It was on the *Times* best-seller list for fourteen weeks, reaching the number-7 position. Bantam produced seven printings of *The Goodbye Look* between 1970 and 1972. Bantam also acquired the rights to the titles previously published by Pocket Books, and during 1970-1972 there were more than seventy Bantam printings of backlist and current Ross Macdonalds.

Nobody knows how to make literary success happen. All explanations necessarily indulge in *post hoc ergo propter hoc.* Promotion and marketing can't make a winner. Neither can reviews. If readers like a writer's previous books, they'll probably read the new one. In the case of Ross Macdonald there was an incremental effect: the more books he published, the more readers were exposed to them. When he had written a score of novels, he had created the market for his work. The breakthrough with *The Goodbye Look* was actually a response to his total output.*

The success of *The Goodbye Look* was consolidated in 1971 by *The Underground Man,* which received a *Newsweek* cover story and a front-page *New York Times Book Review* notice by Eudora Welty, in which she pronounced it his best novel. *The Underground Man* required six Knopf printings (the first of which was 20,000 copies) and was distributed by the Book-of-the-Month Club. It became Millar's most popular novel, selling 54,000 cloth copies in six months and residing on the *Times* best-seller list for seventeen weeks, reaching number 4. Bantam's first printing was 350,000 copies, and fourteen paperback printings were consumed between 1972 and 1979.

The back-to-back success of *The Goodbye Look* and *The Underground Man* established Lew Archer as a brand name like Travis McGee, Philip Marlowe, Mike Hammer. It also called critical attention to Ross Macdonald, who became the subject of articles in academic journals. Although his final two novels were weaker than the superb books of the Sixties, they sold well—despite some critical complaints about sentimentality and formula writing. *Sleeping Beauty* (1973) went through four Knopf printings and was distributed by the Literary Guild; it was on the *Times* best-seller list for six weeks, but got no higher than number 9. There was only one large Bantam printing. *The Blue Hammer* (1976) had three Knopf printings and was also distributed by the Literary Guild; it required four Bantam printings.

The lessons to be drawn from this record are fairly clear. While Kenneth Millar was writing a dozen of the best detective novels in the American language he was underrated or overlooked by critics and readers. Although it was a response to his total achievement, recognition came late and was a flukey thing. A movie of a seventeen-year-old novel, two *New York Times Book Review* front pages, and the *Newsweek* cover brought him the attention he had earned a decade earlier. An easy moral is that you're nobody until the Sunday *Times* loves you. There are more useful conclusions that bear on the practice of popular fiction in the age of the mass-market paperback.

* In England the switch in publishers from Cassell to Collins with *The Ferguson Affair* in 1961 enlarged the Ross Macdonald audience. Collins publishes the Crime Club series and owns the Fontana paperback line; tits-and-navel Fontana covers moved the books off the racks during the early Seventies.

A serious mystery writer cannot depend on the mystery buffs for sustenance or recognition. Too many of them will read anything. Moreover, many good readers avoid mysteries. Both classes of readers have to be told what's good. Publishers place great store in word-of-mouth advertising; but the word about Ross Macdonald filtered down from the top. Only after he attracted official critical attention—as distinguished from notices in the mystery-and-suspense shopping lists—did his books reach the general or cross-section audience Kenneth Millar had been seeking all along.

There may be no such thing as a democratic literature, because literature requires an aristocracy of equipped readers. The crowd has its own crowd-pleasers. Even when Ross Macdonald was being read by both the common reader and the uncommon reader, he was appealing to overlapping—but separate—constituencies. Perhaps that is what democratic literature really means.

George Sims

The Dark Backward

The books on my list of twenty favorite mystery novels would all be by American authors. I have never been interested in "a classic closed community of suspects" or stories with trick endings or revelations on the last page. I want characters who come to life as you read, a sense of reality, atmosphere, emotion and excitement and I find them much more often in the suspense novels written on the other side of the Atlantic.

My list would begin with Dashiell Hammett's famous book *The Maltese Falcon* and include a number of other well known novels such as W.R. Burnett's *The Asphalt Jungle* (the filmed version of this, directed by John Huston, would be on my list of twenty favorite movies), Stanley Ellin's *The Eighth Circle,* William McGivern's *The Big Heat* (another favorite movie, with an unforgettable confrontation between Glenn Ford and Lee Marvin), George V. Higgins's *The Friends of Eddie Coyle* and *The Defection of A.J. Lewinter* by Robert Littell. But I should also include some crime novels which I believe have been unjustly neglected: Ira Wolfert's subtle book *Tucker's People* (again made into a brilliant movie called *The Force of Evil,* starring John Garfield), Robert Knowlton's *Court of Crows,* Thomas Walsh's *Nightmare in Manhattan,* Eleazar Lipsky's *The People Against O'Hara* and Herbert Lieberman's *City of the Dead.* My list would end chronologically with Andrew Coburn's *Off Duty* but on grounds of merit it would be close to the top of the list.

Dashiell Hammett would be represented by two books on the list, *The Maltese Falcon* and *The Glass Key.* Ross Macdonald wrote, "we all came out from under Hammett's black mask," and for me

Hammett is the Master. Any talented writer could base an interesting or amusing character on Hammett's famous "fat man," but to create originals like Caspar Gutman ("the fat man was flabbily fat with bulbous pink cheeks and lips and chins and neck, with a great soft egg of a belly that was all his torso, and pendant cones for arms and legs"), Joel Cairo and Sam Spade takes more than talent. As Raymond Chandler wrote of Hammett, "he wrote scenes that seemed never to have been written before."

Chandler, too, would probably be represented by two books on the list but choosing them would be difficult. The problem is that I like parts of various books by Chandler very much indeed but two favorite titles do not spring to mind readily as they do with Hammett. And my critical judgment might well be influenced by my memories of the Chandler movies. I should find it very difficult to erase images of Humphrey Bogart as Philip Marlowe in *The Big Sleep,* sweating out his interview in the greenhouse with General Sternwood, fending off the foolish Carmen and grinning wolfishly at Mrs. Regan.

Reviewing my favorite suspense novels I see how many of them have one factor in common, that the mysteries stem from events that occurred way back in the past. In *The Tempest* Prospero asks Miranda, "What seest thou else in the dark backward and abysm of time?" I must admit to being fascinated by the past and some friends might say that I am obsessed with it: old songs, old movies, old discs, old photographs and much else to do with "all the dearly beloved," all those human beings who have lived and died. In *The Maltese Falcon* the tricks, lies, treachery and violent deaths stem from the hunt for a "foot-high jewelled bird": "For seventy years, sir, this marvellous item was, as you might say, a football in the gutters of Paris—until 1911 when a Greek dealer named Charilaos Konstantinides found it in an obscure shop. . . ." And in Coburn's book *Off Duty* the foreground is taken up with a hijacked drugs deal, the involvement of the Boston Mafia and the brutal killing of a man, flayed with a bunch of antique keys ("flayed by something that had removed flesh, big bits and pieces, and dislodged an eye"), but the ultimate source of all this violence is the simple fact that years before the two main characters, Rupert Goetz and Frank Chase, had been in love with the same woman.

Many of the books written by Ross Macdonald are bound up with events that took place in the past: his private detective Lew Archer sets out on what appears at first to be a relatively simple case, but the puzzle proves to be complex and leads Archer further and further back in the past. I have fourteen novels by Ross Macdonald on my shelves for favorite thrillers and I find it extremely difficult to select just two or three for my list.

A review of *The Moving Target* by "John Macdonald" (Kenneth Millar's first pseudonym as an author) led me to buy the book within a few weeks of its publication in England in 1951, by Cassell in their "Crime Connoisseur" series. I was attracted by the abrupt start: "The cab turned off U.S. 101 in the direction of the sea. The road looped round the base of a brown hill into a canyon lined with scrub oak. . . ." Then I enjoyed the account of the detective Lew Arless's* first meeting with his crippled client in Carillo Canyon: "Mrs. Sampson looked up from her book. . . . She was half lying on a chaise longue with her back to the late morning sun, a towel draped over her body. There was a wheelchair standing beside her, but she didn't look like an invalid. She was very lean and brown, tanned so dark her flesh seemed hard. Her hair was bleached, curled tightly on her narrow head like blobs of whipped cream. Her age was as hard to tell as the age of a figure carved from mahogany."

Mrs. Sampson's tart quips appealed to me. On two divorced friends: "Millicent and Clyde are dreadfully sordid, don't you think? These aesthetic men! I've always suspected his mistress wasn't a woman." Lew Arless is shown a photograph of Mr. Sampson, the missing millionaire husband: "The face in the leather folder was fat, with thin grey hair and a troubled mouth. The thick nose tried to be bold and succeeded in being obstinate. The smile that folded the puffed eyelids and creased the sagging cheeks was fixed and forced. I'd seen such smiles in mortuaries on the false face of death. It reminded me that I was going to grow old and die." Mrs. Sampson commented on it: "A poor thing, but mine own."

The wisecracks in *The Moving Target* seemed to me to be up to Raymond Chandler's high standard, but I thought that "John Macdonald" could sometimes draw an even more telling vignette. In the second chapter there is a good example of this, a description of Miss Sampson (the missing man's daughter) and Alan Taggart (his pilot) together in a swimming pool: "The pool was on the upper terrace, an oval of green water set in blue tile. A girl and a boy were playing tag, cutting the water like seals. The girl was chasing the boy. He let her catch him. Then they were a man and a woman, and the

* Archer was "Arless" in the Cassell edition.

moving scene froze in the sun. Only the water moved, and the girl's hands. She was standing behind him with her arms round his waist. Her fingers moved over his ribs gently as a harpist's, clenched in the tuft of hair in the centre of his chest. Her face was hidden against his back. His face held pride and anger like a blind bronze. He pushed her hands down and stepped away. Her face was naked then and terribly vulnerable. . . ."

Minor characters are sketched in with economy but their images tend to remain in the mind. "The Filipino servant moved unobtrusively across the patio. Felix's steady smile was a mask behind which his personality waited in isolation, peeping furtively from the depths of his bruised-looking eyes. I had the feeling that his pointed ears heard everything I said, counted my breathing, and could pick up the beat of my heart. . . ."

This is the description of Arless's first encounter with Puddler, an ex-boxer: "The hand missed the bowl (of salted peanuts) and scrabbled in the grass like a crippled lobster. Then he turned his head, and I saw the side of his face . . . it wasn't the face the man in the scarlet shirt had started out with. It was a stone face hacked out by a primitive sculptor. It told a very common twentieth-century story: too many fights, too many animal guts, not enough brains. . . . He was no taller than I was, and he wasn't as wide as the door, but he gave that impression. He made me nervous, the way you feel talking to a strange bulldog on his master's property. . . . I didn't like the way he moved towards me. His left shoulder was forward and his chin in, as if every hour of his day was divided into twenty three-minute rounds. . . ." It is such writing that makes me endorse what Eudora Welty wrote of Ross Macdonald, that he had "the perspective that comes of precise observation and irony."

I also enjoyed the way in which the story moved about in California, from "Santa Teresa" to Hollywood and Pacific Palisades, and that each time "the scene was as vivid as paint." Other minor characters depicted in Hollywood are real enough to walk off the page; a contract writer for Metro: "An ex-reporter from Chicago who had sold his first novel to Metro and never written another, Hunt was turning from a hopeful kid to a nasty old man with the migraine and a swimming pool he couldn't use because he was afraid of the water. I had helped him lose his second wife to make way for his third, who was no improvement. . . ."

But the finest word portrait seemed to me to be that of the psychic, aging film actress Fay Estabrook (played by Shelley Winters in the movie): ". . . In her dowdy costume—black hat with a widow's veil and plain black coat—her big, handsome body looked awkward and ungainly. It may have been the sun in my eyes or simple romanticism, but I had the feeling that the evil which hung in the studio air like an odorless gas was concentrated in that heavy black figure wandering up the empty factitious street. . . . In the Hollywood Roosevelt bar she complained of the air and said she felt wretched and old. Nonsense, I told her, but we moved to the Zebra Room. . . . In the Zebra Room she accused the man at the next table of looking at her contemptuously. I suggested more air. She drove down Wilshire as if she was trying to break into another dimension. . . . She quarrelled with the Ambassador barman on the grounds that he laughed at her when he turned his back. . . . The lady passed out again. At least she said nothing. It was a lonely drive down the midnight boulevard with her half-conscious body. In the spotted coat it was like a sleeping animal beside me in the seat, a leopard or a wildcat heavy with age. It wasn't really old—fifty at most—but it was full of the years, full and fermenting with bad memories. She's told me a number of things about herself, but not what I wanted to know, and I was too sick of her to probe deeper. The one sure thing I knew about her she hadn't had to tell me: she was bad company for Sampson or any incautious man. Her playmates were dangerous. . . ."

There is a really masterful scene where Arless deliberately gets Mrs. Estabrook drunk: "The second drink fixed her. Her face went to pieces as if by its own weight. Her eyes were dull and unblinking. Her mouth hung open in a fixed yawn, the scarlet lips contrasting with the pink-and-white interior. She brought it together numbly and whispered: 'I don't feel so good.' . . . The waitress held the door open with a condoling smile for Mrs. Estabrook and sharp glance for me. Mrs. Estabrook stumbled across the sidewalk like an old woman leaning on a cane that wasn't there. I held her up on her anesthetized legs. . . ."

And another brilliant scene takes place when Mrs. Estabrook passes out once more, when she is in her house, alone with Arless: "'I can't think of anything I want to drink,' she whined. 'Don't let me fall.' I put one arm round her shoulders, which were almost as wide as mine. She leaned hard against me. I felt the stir and swell of her breathing, gradually slowing down. 'Don't try to do anything to me, honey, I'm dead tonight. Some other night. . . .' Her voice was soft and somehow girlish, but blurred. Blurred like the submarine glints of youth in her eyes. Her eyes closed. I could see the faint tremor of her heart-beat in the veins of her withering eyelids. Their fringe of curved dark lashes was a vestige of youth and beauty which made her ruin seem final and hard. It was easier to feel sorry for her when she was sleeping. . . ."

So, *The Moving Target* is a "must" for my list. It led to me tracking down the only other book then available by Kenneth Millar in Britain, *Blue City*, published by Cassell in 1949. Once more I was attracted by the deceptively simple opening paragraph: "All the time you've been away from a town where you lived when you were a kid, you think about it and talk about it as if the air were sweeter in the nostrils than other air. When you meet a man from that town you feel a kind of brotherhood with him, till the talk runs down and you can't remember any more names."

But though the descriptive writing in *Blue City* was effective the story seemed more stereotyped than *The Moving Target* and I found some of the violence gratuitous (which led to a Bostonian critic describing it as "Very, very tough. Not for delicate stomachs!") so it will not find a place on my list.

More reluctantly I also pass over some of the early titles by "John Ross Macdonald": *The Drowning Pool, The Way Some People Die, The Ivory Grin* and *Experience With Evil**. Along with the author's sensitivity, irony and descriptive powers I discerned in these books what the Germans call *Weltschmerz,* a sadness of the world, which I found sympathetic. More than most writers in the genre Ross Macdonald, in his essays, has put his finger on the attraction of such novels. He wrote: "Perhaps, like Mithridates sampling his daily poison, we swallow our regular quotas of fictitious fear and danger in order to strengthen our minds against the real thing. Perhaps we need to be reminded that our planet is an uncertain and unsafe place. . . ."

Again while wearing his other hat, that of the perceptive essayist, Ross Macdonald wrote of the mystery novel writer: "He can lie in wait . . . against the day when another book will haunt him like a ghost rising out of both the past and the future." *The Galton Case* (published by Cassell in 1960) begins in the late nineteen-fifties when the dying Mrs. Galton hires Lew Archer to find her long-lost son, Anthony. It has a simple but effective opening paragraph: "The law

* The British title for *Meet Me At the Morgue.*

offices of Wellesley and Sable were over a savings bank on the main street of Santa Teresa. Their private elevator lifted you from a bare little lobby into an atmosphere of elegant simplicity. It created the impression that after years of struggle you were rising effortlessly to your natural level, one of the chosen."

The Galton case looks hopeless at the start and is described as such by the lawyer, Gordon Sable, who first interviews Archer, for the son had been missing for over twenty years: "The son's name is, or was, Anthony Galton. He dropped out of sight in 1936. He was twenty-two at the time, just out of Stanford. . . ." Archer's comment is: " 'That's a long time ago.' From where I sat, it was like a previous century." But the book does not only deal with events that had taken place in 1936, it goes back yet another decade "to the lawless twenties and the notorious Lempi gang."

The Galton Case contains a dozen brief but brilliant descriptions of the characters that Lew Archer encounters on his quest: "The houseman came up closer to me and smiled. His smile was wide and raw, like a dog's grin, and meaningless, except that it meant trouble. His face was seamed with the marks of the trouble-prone. He invited violence, as certain other people invited friendship." And this is the description of Mr. Culotti, a car-dealer: "A grey-haired man came out, looking cheaply gala in an ice-cream suit. His face was swarthy and pitted like an Epstein bronze, and its two halves didn't quite match. When I got closer to him, I saw that one of his brown eyes was made of glass. He looked permanently startled."

The plot of *The Galton Case* is complicated and involves the discovery of a headless skeleton and "the fabulous Galton rubies which disappeared with the runaway," and a boy's claim to be the son of the missing Anthony Galton. But Ross Macdonald effortlessly draws all these threads together in what the Cassell blurb-writer justly called "an intriguing and brilliantly worked out climax." The book is a strong contender for my list.

I think however that *The Underground Man,* published in England by Collins in 1971, is an even stronger contender. (Ross Macdonald wrote: "Detective fiction can remind us that we are all underground men making a brief transit from darkness to darkness.") In this book Lew Archer is again involved in a case that reaches back into the past, "a web of murder and extortion stretching back through fifteen years," but it also contains a haunting description of a tragic fire that ravages a hillside community in Southern California.

The reader finds a subtle hint of what is to come in the opening paragraph: "A rattle of leaves woke me some time before dawn. A hot wind was breathing in at the bedroom window. I got up and closed the window and lay in bed and listened to the wind." The fifth paragraph contains another prophetic image: "It was a bright September morning. The edge of the sky had a yellowish tinge like cheap paper darkening in the sunlight. There was no wind at all now, but I could smell the inland desert and feel its heat."

Poetical descriptions of the fire paint a dramatic backcloth against which the mystery is solved: "Sparks and embers were blowing down the canyon, plunging into the trees behind the house like bright exotic birds taking the place of the birds that had flown. . . . Smoke hung over the city, giving it a sepia tint like an old photograph. We climbed out of the cars and looked back at the house. The fire bent round it like the fingers of a hand, squeezing smoke out of the windows and then flame. . . . The hillside path was littered with black sticks and grey ashes. . . . I passed the place where the stable had been. The burned-out body of Stanley's convertible was sitting in the open, its tireless rims sunk in the ashes of the building. It looked like a relic of an ancient civilization, ruined and diminished by the passage of centuries, already half buried among their droppings. . . ."

The fire scenes have the authenticity of hard won experience but they are rivalled by the word portraits of people. This is Mrs. Crandall, living in Pacific Palisades: "On a palm-lined street in a kind of Tudor manor with a peaked roof and brown obtruding half-timbers. . . . A blonde woman in black opened the ornately carved door. Her body was so trim against the light that I thought for a moment she was a girl. Then she inclined her head to look at me, and I saw that time had faintly touched her face and begun to tug at her throat. . . Her speech was carefully correct, as if she had taken lessons in talking. I suspected that her natural speech was a good deal rougher and freer. . . . Her body fell into a beautiful still pose, but her faintly pinched face seemed bored with it, or resentful, like an angel living with an animal."

And this is her husband: "Lester Crandall came into the room as if he was the visitor, not I. He was a short heavy-bodied man with iron grey hair and sideburns which seemed to pincer his slightly crumpled face and hold it for inspection. His smile was that of a man who wanted to be liked. His handshake was firm and I noticed that his hands were large and misshapen. They bore the old marks of heavy work: swollen knuckles, roughened skin. He had spent his life, I thought, working his way to the top of a small hill which his daughter had abandoned in one jump. . . . He was like a man with his eyes closed trying to put his hands on a girl that wasn't there. I began to think I had a glimmering of the problem. It was often the same problem—an unreality so bland and smothering that the children tore loose and impaled themselves on the spikes of any reality that offered. Or made their own unreality with drugs."

I also have to include *The Blue Hammer* (the last Ross Macdonald mystery novel, published in England by Collins in 1976) on my list. Lew Archer is hired by Ruth Biemeyer, the wife of a copper magnate, to find a stolen painting, but really he has to solve a number of mysteries and—gradually—"is drawn into a web of family complications and masked brutalities stretching back fifty years through a world where money talks or buys silence. . . ." The stolen canvas was the work of an artist Richard Chantry who had himself been missing for 25 years when the story opens. At one point Archer says, "This case was started in 1943. It's time it was closed."

This is the author's description of one locale: "The University had been built on an elevated spur of land that jutted the sea and was narrowed at its base by a tidal slough. Almost surrounded by water and softened by blue haze, it looked from the distance like a medieval fortress town. Close up, the buildings shed this romantic aspect. They were half-heartedly modern, cubes and oblongs and slabs that looked as if the architect had spent his life designing business buildings."

A number of the descriptions, written in a few lines, are as effective as Imagist poems: ". . . I could see the harbor in the distance. Its masts and cordage resembled a bleached winter grove stripped of leaves and gauntly beautiful. The candle flames reflected in the windows seemed to flicker like St. Elmo's fire around the distant masts. . . . Below the house the sea thumped and fumbled like a dead man trying to climb back into life. I shivered."

In *The Blue Hammer* the author's comments on men and women seem to me like the distillation of a lifetime largely spent in trying to understand them: "Looking into Paolo's opaque black eyes, I thought that the grief you share with women was most always partly desire. At least sometimes you could take them to bed, I thought, and exchange a temporary kindness, which priests were denied. . . . My chosen study was other men, hunted men in rented rooms, aging boys clutching at manhood before night fell and they grew suddenly old. If you were the therapist, how could you need therapy? If you were the hunter, you couldn't be hunted. Or could you. . . . She tapped the floor with her toe, and her whole body moved. She was one of those women whose sex had aged into artiness but might still flare up if given provocation. . . . She moved to unlatch the outer door. Until then, she hadn't shown her age. She was lame, and her hips moved awkwardly. I was reminded of certain kinds of pelagic birds that move at ease in the air or on the ocean, but have a hard time walking. Her white head was like a bird's. It was sparse and elegant, with hollow cheeks, a thin straight nose, eyes that still had distance and wildness. She caught me looking at her, and smiled. One of her front teeth was missing. It gave her a gamine touch."

The plot of *The Blue Hammer* is extremely complicated, perhaps too much so to be readily followed, and this leads to a kind of Dickensian ploy in Chapter XLI where Lew Archer recapitulates: "I sat in my car in the failing afternoon and tried to straighten out the case in my mind. It had started with the trouble between two brothers, Richard Chantry and his illegitimate half-brother. It appeared that Richard had stolen William's work and William's girl. . . ." Despite this complexity the reader is carried along by the author's skill and some brilliant scenes, like the one in the following chapter in which Archer confronts Mrs. Chantry: "Francine had been living for decades deep in the knowledge of murder. It was beginning to show in her face and body, reaching up for her from the earth like gravity. . . . Her jaw was slack and grim, her eyes dull. But she held on to her bag the way a plunging fullback holds the ball. . . . 'Were you in an accident?' 'I don't really know what happened. I was trying to get off the freeway, and things went out of control all of a sudden. That seems to be the story of my life!' Her laughter was like a dry compulsive cough . . . there was a note of terror in Francine Chantry's voice. She sounded like a woman who had stepped off the edge of the world and discovered too late that she could never step back. When we got into my car and entered the freeway, the sense of moving through empty space stayed with me. We seemed to be flying above the rooftops of the tract houses that lined the freeway on both sides. . . ."

No, I can't relinquish *The Blue Hammer* as a favorite mystery novel but neither can I discard *The Moving Target, The Galton Case* or *The Underground Man*—so I must re-plan my list to make room for four titles by Ross Macdonald.

Robert B. Parker

Heroes and Debts

I never met him personally. I knew him through Lew Archer, and I knew him as Ross Macdonald. But I owe him, as does every one of us who step, albeit less gracefully, to the same drumbeat. For in his craft and his integrity he made the detective form a vehicle for high seriousness. It is not that others hadn't tried, it was that he succeeded.

In novel after novel Ross Macdonald examined the things that matter most: the painful difficulty of love, the ceaseless way in which yesterday distorts today, the pressing need for someone who cares and is strong enough to matter. Archer was both caring and strong, and he carried in himself, flawed and often weary, the apotheosis of the form.

It is a form, Macdonald once said, "rigid as a sonnet." In saying so he was suggesting that form is not limitation but possibility, and he was correct of course. But he knew, I am sure, as most of us do, that the form in which he worked is not a sequence of events, or a way of telling, or even a pattern of adventure. The form of the private eye novel is simply the belief in a hero. Lew Archer *is* the form, as Marlowe was.

All of us who glean where Macdonald reaped begin where he began, with the vision of a man rooted in romance, a man with mythic potential, capable of cruelty when necessary and compassion when possible; hard, isolate, stoic, and, unavoidably upon occasion, a killer. Macdonald invigorated that hero, committed him to finding lost children and salvaging lost hopes and mending broken families. Macdonald showed us that honor and compassion could be extended in ways that no detective writer had ever extended them, and he did it in stories so strong, and prose so supple and clean that he made the world of literary judgment pay attention.

It was not just that Ross Macdonald taught us how to write; he did something much more, he taught us how to read, and how to think about life, and, maybe, in some small, but mattering way, how to live.

Richard Layman

Out From Under Hammett's Black Mask

Ross Macdonald respected the value of antecedents: truth is in the past; sons bear their fathers' legacies. He was preoccupied with the importance the search for identity plays in people's lives, and he paid ample homage to his own literary forebears in the course of exploring the traditions he wrote from. He was smoother, better educated, more enlightened than the men who pioneered the type of novel he wrote, but still the most important fact about him may well be that he was a second-generation hard-boiled mystery writer.

The first generation was presided over by a sickly autodidact with a talent for writing and first-hand experience that bolstered his tales about a faceless detective working in a city afflicted by moral anarchy. In 1922 he began writing detective stories for a pulp magazine called *Black Mask;* within a decade, he was being called the father of a literary movement. His name was Dashiell Hammett, and his genius was that he took an unpliable literary form and devised a method for bending it to reflect realistically the malaise of American society in the postwar era. Hammett's innovations were modest, really, yet they struck at the heart of the distinction that separates mystery writers from authors, potboilers from belles lettres. Hammett's achievement as a writer was not that he wrote dialogue in street vernacular, nor that he popularized the professional detective, nor that he shifted the focus of his writing from unusual crimes committed by unlikely suspects to an accurate depiction of the criminal underworld, nor even that he concocted an ideal blend of form, style, and material. Those elements are incidental to the quality that has caused his work to endure. Hammett is remembered today because he discarded the notion that mystery fiction has literary limitations. He wrote as if he were oblivious to the restrictions other writers had accepted as inherent in fiction which has a detective for a protagonist and a murder mystery for its plot.

Hard-boiled writing always showed the quality of taking itself seriously—often too seriously; and there is something endemic in hard-boiled detective fiction that gave it the capability that the Golden Age mystery lacked of transcending genre fiction. The premise of Hammett's brand of hard-boiled detective fiction was that corruption is a human condition, and the best one can do is to come to terms with it. Coming to terms with corruption may mean violently opposing corrupt people; it may mean forming an alliance with the forces of corruption in the interest of self-preservation; it may require a self-sufficient person to protect innocent people from being victimized; or it may involve a man discovering what is corrupt in himself and struggling against it. The protagonist must confront the flaws in man's nature—the forces that drive him to murder, steal, pillage, and plunder; to the abuse of power and the misuse of the public trust.

The hard-boiled detective was a loner, set apart from polite society by his knowledge of the alley-ways, separated from the underworld by his code. He was most effective when he worked apart from any organization, because he had to exercise his hazardous freedom wherever it led, unfettered by legal obfuscations, moral preconceptions, or agency rules. He was guided by situation ethics based on an entirely personal sense of right and wrong. He had to be sufficiently altruistic—or at least principled—to pursue his occupation despite its meager material rewards; he had to be calloused enough to withstand the emotional trauma of unrelenting violence and injustice; most difficult, he had to operate in the criminal underworld without being totally corrupted by his associations. Simply put, he was an existential man searching for truth in a world complicated by the violence that results from moral confusion.

At its best, hard-boiled detective fiction was modern tragedy. The focus was not on the victim, but on the criminal, who demonstrated a sort of tragic flaw common to society. The burden of the tragedy was borne by the detective, who typically narrated the tale, acting as both chorus and hero. Physically, he was invulnerable; spiritually, though, he was jaded by the awesome knowledge that his job, which was to bring order to a chaotic world, could never be completed. He was a seedy Sisyphus afflicted with an unrealizable moral vision.

Hammett fathered an unruly brood of writers with uneven talents. Because the hard-boiled hero was subject to the pressures of traditional ethics, criminal anarchy, prejudice, pride, and vengeance, it was easy for him to become distorted into a fantasy figure who acted out our basest daydreams about crude, selfish, myopic justice; because of the worldly burden he bore, the luxury of resigned self-pity was sometimes too great a temptation for him to resist. Indeed, most hard-boiled detective fiction has been marred by such distortions of character, which have led to moral oversimplifications and facile views of social relationships. Hammett's literary legacy has often been squandered. The superficial qualities of his writing have been shamelessly exploited, yet that central vision of his that saw pure art in the detective novel has rarely been explored.

Ross Macdonald inherited Hammett's vision and honored it. He provided the same example for writers after World War II that Hammett did for writers of the Jazz Age. In his mature work, Macdonald stripped away the floss from hard-boiled writing and got to the heart of the matter—an insular detective searching for truth by investigating the mysteries that confront him, struggling in the process to understand the forces that shape him. Macdonald expanded the tradition Hammett fathered in his depiction of an investigator driven by an obsession to learn the truth about what happens, why it happens, and what its implications are. Lew Archer feels a moral compulsion to understand his cases because he realizes that he is a participant in the dreadful humanity he observes. For him criminal investigation is introspection. This is how Macdonald altered the hard-boiled novel: he turned it inward so that instead of combating the effects of aberrant behavior, his detective explores its causes, describing in the process a complex set of associations among people and between people and their environment.

"I've been trying to put into my books the same sorts of things that a reader finds in the general novel," Macdonald once said, "a whole version of life in our society and in our time." Few writers in this century have attempted as much, and no other has chosen the form of the detective novel. Hammett mapped out the territory and showed by example that it was without artistic limits; Macdonald created a full fictional world, richly symbolical, which both mirrors reality and elucidates it.

"After I served my apprenticeship to Hammett and Raymond Chandler, I had to learn to write my own kind of novel," Macdonald stated. And so it has been, the present an extension of the past. Lew Archer is his hard-boiled father's son, and Ross Macdonald, assured by the awareness of his place in a literary tradition, has achieved what Hammett imagined.

William Goldman

The Macdonald Conspiracy

What happened to Ross Macdonald on that long ago summer morning was anything but a mystery. Rather, it was a carefully plotted and reasonably well brought off conspiracy. A conspiracy of fans.

All of it made possible by the power of the *Times.*

The end of the 1960s was a particularly effervescent period in the history of *The New York Times Book Review.* There was so much money around that the staff kept expanding and so did the number of pages of the supplement. And if, for example, a member of the staff was genuinely enthusiastic about devoting prominent space to a novelist who wasn't French or German or weirdly Latin American, the editor might say, "Oh well, go ahead," and a lengthy piece of criticism would be commissioned.

There is little doubt that the single most important position for a book to be commented on in this country is the front page of the *Sunday Book Review.* Maybe a *Time* or a *Newsweek* cover story is worth more, but then again, maybe not. And in any case, those are rare. This was as true in '69 as it is today.

But in '69, there was a fillip.

If the *Review* was totally behind a book, if it felt it was pushing something of genuine import, the front page review ran over to the second page—

—and on page two began a long interview with the author.

This double-barrelled assault—the "Good Housekeeping Seal of Approval" *twice*—was often enough to rocket a writer from obscurity to, literally, overnight fame. (Page two is now taken up with an ad, so none of this is possible today.)

But in the Spring of '69, *Slaughterhouse Five* was given that double treatment and catapulted Kurt Vonnegut, rightfully, from the position of a cult figure whispered about on college campuses to his present eminence.

Another event of that '69 Spring was this: *The Goodbye Look* was sent out to various periodicals and newspapers for coverage.

The conspiracy was about to begin.

Since the Archer novels dealt with the past as much as the present, it seems fitting now to go back a few years in time. Three years, to be precise. And to a man reading a book on a porch.

That man was John Leonard and he was the initial conspirator. In 1966 Leonard was unemployed, working on a novel, and acting as houseparent while his then wife completed her graduate work.

The family was located in a small apartment in a small Massachusetts town, across the Charles River from Harvard. It was an academic community and academics, then and now, are notorious for trading books with each other. Leonard knew a number of people in the area, and while not an academic himself, was involved with the trading.

And so, one afternoon while his baby daughter slept, he sat on the porch of his apartment and began to read *The Chill*.

His reaction, when he finished, was rather more positive than otherwise: "Holy shit," he remembers thinking, "this is the real stuff. The family secret is a great theme. My God, this is a work of American Literature."

Not long afterwards, he took a job working for *The Sunday New York Times Book Review*.

Back to the Spring of '69 now, and the arrival of *The Goodbye Look* at the *Times*. Leonard wanted to do something special for it. But he needed help. So he went to Walter Clemons, who was new to the *Review* staff, and asked him if he had ever read any Ross Macdonald.

Clemons, who was to become the second conspirator, had not. But he had heard favorable reports. Leonard requested Clemons to pick up a few Archer novels and read them to see if their opinions coincided. Clemons set out to buy the books.

Not all that easy.

Eventually, he ended up going to eighteen different bookstores around the city before finally managing to round up half a dozen.

The Chill did it for him, too. (Clemons feels that *The Chill* is the one that does it for most people.) He read the books quickly and met with Leonard; they were in agreement—Macdonald was no more a simple writer of hard-boiled detective novels than Vonnegut was a man who turned out off-beat science fiction.

What they hoped for, the two of them, was major space in the magazine. Leonard was about to leave the *Sunday Book Review* and take over the job of daily book reviewer of the *Times*. As a kind of going away present, he was granted the right to take a trip and interview a writer.

He wanted to interview Ross Macdonald.

To get their hoped-for major space, they needed one thing: absolute assurance that the review of *The Goodbye Look* would be strongly positive.

Clemons said: "I can promise that."

The reason for his certainty was that I had known Clemons for a number of years and whenever the subject of books came up, I would hock him to for chrissakes read some Ross Macdonald. I'd also done the screenplay of the first Archer novel, *The Moving Target*, which became the movie, *Harper*.

Clemons called and explained the situation. I told him two things: (1) there was no way I would miss the chance of reviewing the book and (2) there wasn't going to be a lot negative in anything I wrote.

I was now the third conspirator.

Thus protected, Leonard and Clemons met with the editor of the *Review* and presented their case. They said that Macdonald was an important and overlooked writer of serious novels and worthy of attention. Francis Brown, the editor, would probably have gone along with them in any case. But the specifics here made it even more difficult for him to reject them: Leonard was about to leave and Clemons had just arrived, and saying "no" would have left a sour taste with one, would have more than likely deflated the other.

Brown gave his go ahead, and before I had even finished reading *The Goodbye Look*, Leonard was on a plane to California.

Probably everyone who's tried to write knows it isn't easy money at the brick factory. Speaking personally, I don't think I ever sweated more than during the two week period it took to complete the Macdonald review.

First of all, outside of school, I'd never written a book review before. And this was going to be for the *Sunday Times*, out there in front of God and everybody.

That was the easy part: what assaulted me continually was my passion for the author. I had been a lunatic Archer fan since 1950, when I picked up John Macdonald's *The Moving Target* from a crummy book rack in the equally crummy bus station in Elyria, Ohio.

Over the next two decades, obviously I'd read all the Archer books, and I was convinced that not only was I reading one of my favorite novelists, I was reading the work of Someone Very Special.

I remember once when I was in the army and I met another Macdonald nut, (a Ph.D., yet). We talked for hours and my most clear memory of the encounter was how furtive it was: Dreiser was a Novelist then, and so was Buck and so was Thomas Wolfe. And here we were whispering that this so-called writer of tough guy whodunits was superior to any of them. (Thirty years ago, you just didn't say that kind of thought out loud.)

To write what I felt so passionately to be true panicked me. Because on top of everything else, I didn't think *The Goodbye Look* was the best Macdonald. Not for me as fine as *The Zebra Striped Hearse*, say, or *Black Money*. And certainly not in a class with *The Chill*.

When I had finally finished, I met with Clemons for dinner at the much missed Manny Wolff's restaurant. (The best filet in town.) I gave him the review and while he read it, I walked around and around the block. When I returned he looked pleased. "I think this will do fine," was all he said.

Now placement became crucial.

The *Times* worked then on a two-week lead time, and then as now, editors go with the best they've got. They had my review and Leonard's interview, and there was no question they would run them.

Someplace.

Maybe in the middle, maybe toward the back. But if something better came in—a review of a known and significant writer—there is no way Kenneth Millar would have been given what he got: all of pages one and two and half of page nineteen.

Leonard was, if anything, even more positive than I was. I said Macdonald was "One of the best American novelists now operating" and that the Archer books were "the finest series of detective novels ever written by an American."

Leonard wrote this: "Ten years ago, while nobody was looking—or rather, while everybody was looking in the wrong direction—a writer of detective stories turned into a major American novelist."

That double salvo did it—maybe four thousand words raving about Ross Macdonald changed his career. *The Goodbye Look* became a best seller, as have all his novels since. Succeeding help from high places—a *Newsweek* cover, a famous Eudora Welty review, again on the front page of the *Times* two years later—cemented what had begun that first Sunday in June.

Those of us who loved Macdonald's work were safe to come out of the closet now. No need for furtiveness any more.

There is a feeling prevalent among many, that very good work—truly excellent writing—will eventually out. The real question is whether it's going to out soon enough for the author to benefit from it.

Because of the conspiracy, thank God, Macdonald benefited when he was very much around.

I said at the beginning that this was not a mystery, but that is not entirely true—there is one point that will never be known. Leonard has absolutely no idea who the person was that lent him, to help him through baby-sitting, the copy of *The Chill.*

But whoever and wherever you are, a lot of us are grateful.

The power of the *Times,* as stated, is the hero of this piece. Or secondary hero, I should say. Because the novels are the magic. And they were with us long before that June morning thirteen years ago. And they are with us now.

And always, always will be. . . .

Gilbert Sorrentino

Ross Macdonald:
Some Remarks on the Limitation of Form

It is surely not an original observation to note that *The Blue Hammer,* Ross Macdonald's last novel, is an oblique, a kind of subtle completion of that which was adumbrated in the first Lew Archer novel, *The Moving Target,* though the later book is at once more complex, less rhetorically gaudy, and reliant on metonymy rather than metaphor for its scaffolding. *The Blue Hammer* works, that is, vertically rather than horizontally—the missing Chantry painting is not analogous to anything nor does it function as a symbol; on the contrary, it is a sign, a correlative, for the evil, waste, and betrayal that the novel uncovers, or, perhaps more precisely, that the past gives up. Macdonald goes so far as to give us a clue to his recuperative intentions by referring, in *The Blue Hammer,* to the death, in *The Moving Target,* of the thug, Puddler, at Archer's hands. This passing fragment of information is absolutely irrelevant to the solution of the mystery, and is placed into the text so as to call attention to itself and to its author's conception of his evolving work.

2.

We do a disservice to Macdonald's writings by considering them as outside the quite rigid and artificial structure of the detective novel. Ross Macdonald nowhere surpassed or transcended the limitations of the form in which he chose to work. He worked brilliantly *within* the rigors of this form. That is his strength and valor as a writer.

The detective novel is as thoroughly locked into its form as are the sonnet or the ode, and it is comprehensible or intelligible only in the context of its history. Macdonald can be clearly "seen" as a descendant of Hammett and Chandler, and they are understandable only insofar as they exist within the tradition of the ratiocinative story as defined by Poe. While it may be possible to transcend this form, such transcendence merely takes the detective novel *out of itself,* so that it is no longer the detective novel but something else altogether; as, for instance, one might say that the theater, as a form, has been transcended by the motion picture. Certainly it has—by no longer being theater. Macdonald trusted his form, and was held by it because of what, from *The Galton Case* on, he surely saw were is depthless possibilities and inexhaustible permutations. In an interview, he says: "My books are somewhat limited by the kind of structure and subject matter that is inherent in the contemporary detective novel. I seem to work best within such limitations." I read the phrase "somewhat limited" as a kind of modest irony: it is the "limited" quality of his books that makes them perfect models of a particular kind of fiction, a fiction for which many American critics regularly apologize, or, worse, attempt to make more "serious" by denying that it is this particular kind of fiction—the detective story. Macdonald has often been praised for being better than the genre within which he worked. But it is self-evident that his brilliance as a writer is firmly located in his purity of design: his "ideas" are as unremarkable as those of newspaper editorials—or Christianity.

The French, however, have never taken the detective story lightly, and it is instructive that the *nouveaux romanciers,* most notably Michel Butor and Alain Robbe-Grillet, have used variations on the form as the basis of many of their works, variations that range from the detective as murderer, as in Robbe-Grillet's *The Erasers,* to the layered complexities of present as instant past, as in Butor's *Passing Time.* Of Butor's work, John Sturrock, in *The French New Novel,* writes: "The real detective is now the reader; the narrator assembles the relevant evidence but he is denied the power to conceptualize it."

I don't mean to suggest that Macdonald has done anything of this kind in his novels, although it is apparent that Archer is slowly transformed, from book to book, from the detective who has "the power to conceptualize" to a man who acts as a kind of catalyst by means of whom the evidence inevitably and relentlessly conceptualizes *itself*. He does not so much dig for information as he is led ineluctably to it. The leader of the Society of Mutual Love, in *The Blue Hammer*, says: "You seem to be a man engaged in an endless battle, an endless search. Has it ever occurred to you that the search may be for yourself? And that the way to find yourself is to be still and silent . . .?" And Archer thinks: "They were questions I had asked myself, though never in just those terms." In this final work, Archer, although he asks questions and pokes, prods, and worries recalcitrant and lying characters in his search for truth, is, in a curious but salient way, falling into silence. He talks as much as he did twenty years earlier, but the talk is somehow *given* him by the unfolding corruption that "wants" to be revealed. Murder will out. Archer has been changed from a mere seeker to the midwife who will deliver the original sins that exist at the core of the case.

3.

Ross Macdonald has said: "I once made a case for the theory . . . that much of the modern development of the detective story stems from Baudelaire, his 'dandyism' and his vision of the city as inferno." He might well have gone on to say that the dandy, a pure product of the Decadence, survives, in a basic mode, as the fictional private detective. Baudelaire, in "The Dandy," writes:

> It [dandyism] is the burning need to create an originality for oneself, a need contained within the exterior limits of convention. It is a kind of cult of oneself which may survive the search for happiness to be found in someone else, in woman, for example; which may even survive everything that is called illusion. It is the pleasure of astonishing and the proud satisfaction of never being astonished.

And further: "The characteristic of beauty in the dandy consists especially in the cold attitude which comes from the unbreakable resolution not to be moved; you might call it a latent flame which you guess exists, which might but which will not spread its light." These definitions fit, of course, Lew Archer—and Marlowe, Spade, and the Op as well.

The pertinence of Macdonald's remark becomes more pointed when one recalls that Baudelaire wrote with great perception on Poe, and that one of the aspects of Poe's work that was most admired by Baudelaire was its artificiality, i.e., to Baudelaire, Poe labored to conceal all that might seem spontaneous in his writing, so that all of it appeared to be the product of "cold" intellectualism, far removed from the *bête noire* of the Decadence, the automatic writing of inspiration. In contemporary terms, there are few manifestations of fiction more contrived than the detective novel—Macdonald's being no exception. The beauty of this genre lies in its crystalline balances; there is no way that it can "go where it wants to go." It is a perfect expression of dandyism with a dandy as its hero.

It may also be relevant to Macdonald's acute remark on Baudelaire to note that an important facet of the writing of the Decadence was its fascination with time- and space-exoticism (to distance itself from despised naturalism). In Macdonald's novels, it can be argued that these motifs survive as the looming and secret past and the curious culture of Southern California.

4.

I have said that Macdonald trusted his form. I should add too that nowhere does he mock it, even as he began to rely less and less on Hammett and Chandler. The analogies and comparisons used in his early work are taken from the essential vocabulary of glossy similes and straight-faced ironic locutions that inform the entire genre. Some of these, if not all of them, are from a common fund of tropes and imagery available to all detective-story writers, so that they would be at home, so to speak, in the elegant work of Chandler as well as in the clumsy writing of Spillane. In *The Moving Target,* for instance, we find such flashy comparatives as: "The light blue haze in the lower canyon was like a thin smoke from slowly burning money"; "She made the blood run round in my veins like horses on a track"; "Universal City wore its stucco façades like yellowing paper collars"; "Mrs. Estabrook looked up at us with eyes like dark searchlights"; and, in ironic mood, these contructions: "Her hand grasped his left knee. He let it stay there"; "I wanted to respond to her melancholy look, but I didn't know what to do with my face"; "I made myself uncomfortable on a hard-backed chair against the wall." There are dozens more, all of them givens of the genre. They are the sort of thing that Victor Shklovsky, in "Art as Technique," is thinking of when he writes:

> The more you understand an age, the more convinced you become that the images a given poet used and which you thought his own were taken almost unchanged from another poet. The works of poets are classified or grouped according to the new techniques that poets discover and share, and according to their arrangement and development of the resources of language; poets are much more concerned with arranging images than with creating them.

The conventional phrases noted above are the "images" that Macdonald had to hand during his early career. The novels from *The Galton Case* on, however, reveal "new techniques," and it is the discovery and use of these techniques that make Ross Macdonald without peer in the highly artificial and difficult form in which he worked, a form that constantly begs to collapse into the banal.

By the time we arrive at *The Blue Hammer,* we are in the presence of a prose that is flatter, less ornate, and lacking in the bright analogies and ironies of the earlier books. This novel has removed itself from the surface conventions of the genre, and relies almost wholly on the understructure of complex form for its effects. As I have suggested, the book functions vertically, doing away with the simple metaphors of *The Moving Target* in favor of the dissociative techniques of metonymy. The associative comparative (this is like this and therefore . . .) has been discarded.

While it is fruitless to speculate on that which is unwritten, it is possible that Macdonald might have finally reached a point in his fiction in which the uncovered truths about his shattered and doomed people would show them to be criminal only in the *moral* sense; that is, he may have come to a fiction in which there were no criminals, only victims. He seems to me to have been heading there. His ultimate victim could well have been Lew Archer.

5.

The line linking *The Moving Target* to *The Blue Hammer* can be described as a graph of maturation. This graph reveals that Macdonald neither derided nor cheapened the detective story and the linguistic paraphernalia germane to it. He was, early on, surely aware that it was no more than paraphernalia and he used it, I should guess, because his mentors had shown him that the metaphor is a method whereby the detective story—with its grid of connections—can be most efficaciously constructed. And the structural metaphor can be repeated, *in parvo,* in the quick, bright analogies of the surface. In his early work, Macdonald thought metaphorically, and his novels are made like those of his teachers. He surrendered to the form, and also eschewed the fetish of originality in favor of a position as a wholly serious writer working in a tradition that he honored.

When he came to his own necessity and began to see that his given materials were not things that stood for other things but were, instead, the blinds and masks for the hidden truths that Archer would have, almost unwillingly, thrust upon him, he changed his flashing and associative method for the plainer one that permitted the world and Archer their confusion. Archer ages and becomes wiser but it is a wisdom rooted in the knowledge that the solution to specific mysteries cannot approach the mystery of his own being. He is still essentially the dandy, but his aloofness and control have begun to crack in the face of a world that is just about out of control. He has reached the point at which analogies are simply lies in the presence of such a reality.

Yet he occasionally still gestured toward his teachers, and even in *The Blue Hammer,* a novel whose overwhelming ambience is that of a penetrant greyness, we read such sudden glintings of the "older style" as: "Like a flashing ornament suspended from an infinitely high ceiling, the red-tailed hawk swung over the Biemeyer house," and "The shadows under the trees were as thick and dark as old blood." Those are *hommages* to Hammett and Chandler, no longer necessary to Macdonald, but laid into the text consciously and lovingly.

6.

As with all committed writers, form, for Ross Macdonald, was not something to chafe against but to transmute and develop within its own container. Through his early deference to a rigorous and conventionalized form his later, unconventional art flourished.

Eudora Welty

Finding the Connections

He had always acknowledged and respected his early teachers and influences, but he found his own voice and became a more serious and complex writer than Chandler and Hammett ever were. He pressed his work toward an end far different from what either of them had tried for. *The Galton Case* gave him his true direction and extended his powers to reach a form that satisfied his needs, and brought him Archer. As Ross Macdonald he could work within a form that could contain and make eloquent use of what Kenneth Millar knew best, that is, his own life.

In his essay, "Writing *The Galton Case,*" the author says:

"The literary detective has provided writers since Poe with a disguise, a kind of welder's mask enabling us to handle dangerously hot material." Archer's "semi-transparent presence places the story at one remove from the author. . . . The detective and his story can become means of knowing oneself and saying the unsayable."

Surprise has been expressed sometimes that he was the author of very powerful crime novels in spite of having been a quiet and scholarly man, who earned a doctorate and a Phi Beta Kappa key, who was at one time a college teacher. He wrote the novels, it seems clear, not in spite of his particular equipment but because of it. He explored the possibilities of the crime novel precisely for the uses he could make of its compressed, concentrated dramatic form, to show by means of its speech and action and plot—as complicated and demanding as any plot could be—what he saw, understood, felt about his fellow human beings. Be very sure, he had his finger on our pulse, his eye on our clock, his ear to what we say—and an inner ear not missing what we don't say. He cared about our mutual situation, our mutual chances, our mutual guilt, the ways we are all ending up. The best evidence that this is so is the way he wrote.

He made of the popular spoken language a tool for his very particular use. His sensitivity to the implications of American vernacular was as keen and delicate as Lardner's. When his characters speak, the poverty of their language becomes eloquent of their human frailty, and this is what we hear. We read in their conversations with each other the spiritual loss they have suffered.

It would not be in his nature to "write down" to his wide readership in popular fiction, and this is the opposite of what his vernacular style intends. (Indeed, in the spell of Archer's urgent, fast-moving narration, readers absorb, in passing, words like "demi-urge" and "implosion" and references to the Rorschach test and Zeno's paradox of Achilles and the Tortoise. All pertains to the novel's whole.) Kenneth Millar described himself as a man "in love with the language," and he made his particular use of it an art.

The Macdonald novel begins as a rule at the point of discovery of a crime. The question is not simply, Who did it?—not by a long shot. Where, and from how long ago, out of what human fissure, did this crime start, and why at this moment did it erupt? What connections will lead us back to the source? The identity of the man or woman there to be found can be reached only through following this network of connections. It's the connections that absorb the author and magnetize his plots into their intricate and daunting patterns. In the brilliant, shapely designs of their construction, in their motions, in their timing, in their only seeming coincidences ("There are no coincidences," says Archer), in their evolving whole of moral significance, in their depth of irony, the plots are keyed and attuned to human beings as human beings. The novels' central concern is human relationships—i.e., human beings in trouble.

It is not illogical that Ross Macdonald, a novelist absorbed by character and working through structure, should have found the detective story responsive and flexible to his needs. The mystery and its solution are twin constructions in his hands, based on the same secret, which is always one of serious human import. This secret is often buried in a family past, and it needs to be made known *now*—urgently, in order to save a life, often a child's or a young person's. Thus Archer is driven headlong on his search. To this private detective, spinning through time and the generations as he spins through the hills of California, it is a search for comprehension as well, for understanding. And Macdonald, at the eventual success of the tracking down, lets us see further: uncover the secret and it goes back as far as Sophocles.

Macdonald plots, set on a course of discovery, are strewn—without seeming for an instant to lose momentum—with might-have-beens. For characters, major and minor, are given their due. All, givers and takers, killers and victims, the lost and the found, are qualified participants whom we are to see joined at the meeting point of their lives, lit up and exposed and brought to speak by the sudden flare of crisis. Though the novels carry through the search for the killer, and finally name the killer with strong, often chilling impact, the reader is aware (through Archer's experiencing the story) that the ending is not resolved in a passing of judgment. Character, rather than deed in itself, is what remains uppermost and decisive to Macdonald as a novelist. In the course of its being explained, guilt is seldom seen as flat-out; it is disclosed in the round, and the light and shadings of character define its true features. The history of more than a single character will surface before a crime's true nature is understood, and before the full reach of the crime is comprehended and its roots in the past and the lengths they've traveled lie unearthed.

Archer, carrying out his investigation, driven to solve his case, would always settle for mercy rather than justice. The Macdonald novels over the years have shown more and more an abiding sense of human frailty. His detective speaks to us not as a moralist but as a fellow sufferer.

When a character in *The Far Side of the Dollar* describes a crisis as being "like reality exploding," Archer tells her, ". . . You can't explode reality. Life hangs together in one piece. Everything is connected with everything else. The problem is to find the connections." Once—it comes near the end of *Instant Enemy*—this central idea takes form before us in the sight of the city of Los Angeles at night, a remarkable passage with its intensity characteristically held to a point by the humanity and self-mockery of Archer:

". . . I lived for nights like these, moving across the city's great broken body, making connections among its millions of cells. I had a crazy wish or fantasy that some day before I died, if I made all the right neural connections, the city would come all the way alive. Like the Bride of Frankenstein."

There is an account by the naturalist Louis J. Halle in his book *The Storm Petrel and the Owl of Athena* (Princeton University Press, 1970) of storm petrels he went looking for at their breeding place on the uninhabited island of Mousa in the Shetlands. At the edge of the sea stood a prehistoric fortress, a round tower, known as the Broch of Mousa. He made his approach to this tower in the only hour of that northern summer night when true darkness falls, between one and two in the morning, when the storm petrels would be relieving each other at the nests.

On reaching shore, all the naturalist could make out was the dark face of the wall. There was no sign of life visible. But at the point of greatest darkness, a low sound, of "unplaceable" origin, began to permeate the air. He describes it as continuous, a sort of purring, or snoring sound, interrupted every few seconds with perfect regularity by a single "undescribable" note. He realized in time that this came from within the wall a few inches away from his face. There were, he made out, innumerable chinks in this stone wall, and the air around him now became filled with swirling, incoming, flying shapes. Birds had silently arrived from the sea and were now skimming the face of the wall, darting into those chinks and disappearing, each to his nest in the dark. Those sounds from within, like a whirring watchworks, were signals. The birds fluttered up and down, or horizontally, before it, or kept swinging like pendulums, until they found the one, the right chink, and entered by it.

The storm petrels of Mousa were not aware of the existence of humankind. The naturalist put his hand over one of the birds as it tried to enter one of the chinks and plucked it from the wall. It was gentle in his hand, and its eye looked back at the man, "gentle and indifferent." The man's hand even found its way into a chink and reached a nest, and the egg under the sitting bird's tail was warm.

As the birds from the sea flew in, those from the nests flew out, darting from the wall in a straight line. Within minutes of its release every one of them must have been miles out over the open sea. Then once more not a bird was in sight. "Now one would never guess that inside this stone wall was life, that hearts were beating in there," the account concludes. "Even the watchworks had stopped."

The approach of naturalist and novelist is alike in the call upon intuitiveness, the acute sense of when and where and how to arrive at the moment of discovery. Naturalist and novelist both investigate mystery, and both find some direct affirmation of the phenomena of living—staying alive—in our strange world, each life going out and coming in making its sound, its signal from within, in the dark. The tower with its innumerable hidden nests is as teeming as Los Angeles in its cells of light. And Los Angeles as full of secret life as the tower. I saw them as connected, one riddle.

Exceeding all other connections is of course that of human love. In the crime novel, the murderer, in simplest aspect, is one who breaks his human connection, not only with his victim but with all society. Killer and victim themselves "connect" in crime, finally and fearfully but as certainly as lovers connect in giving and receiving love. In a Macdonald novel, the presence of crime is the story we're being told of the absence of love. All its unfolding of drama, the tracking to its source of a wrong done, discovers at the end its beginning in love's abuse or denial. The pattern is circular.

The novels suggest to us too that the perimeters, the foreshadowings of crime are closer to murder than we know: the lying and coercion and denial in human relationships that can outlast a life's endurance. And the crime novels offer insights into the good at the same time they are dramatically acted out in evil. Indeed the problem of "good" and "bad" characters may coincide, may be the same. As a number of Macdonald novels point out explicitly, it is often the *victim* of a set of circumstances who becomes the murderer.

What Kenneth Millar was signaling to us in these fine and lasting novels is plain and undisguised: find the connections; recognize what they mean; thereby, in all charity, understand.

Ralph B. Sipper

The Last Goodbye

He wasn't clever at all: he merely told
The unhappy Present to recite the Past
Like a poetry lesson till sooner
Or later it faltered at the line where

Long ago the accusations had begun . . .

W. H. AUDEN—IN MEMORY OF SIGMUND FREUD

One spring day in 1981 Kenneth Millar came to my office and in the most dispassionate of tones told me that he could no longer remember things. I was not unduly surprised. The change in Ken, though gradual, had become unmistakable. Where once he would examine our books with pure interest, he now contented himself with idle touching, seldom taking a volume off the shelves. We were working at the time on *Self-Portrait,* his collection of autobiographical essays, and the simple facts of his life which we needed for the book eluded him as he tried to recall them.

I probed for medical details which Ken deflected with less than specific answers. He had consulted doctors; there was an organic basis for his lapses of mind; the prognosis was not good. I soon learned that the disease had a name—Alzheimer's.

Ken had come for a purpose. He asked me to visit his home periodically to keep his papers in order. And he asked me to advise his friends that he could no longer answer their letters. "What shall I tell them?" I asked. "Use your good judgment," Ken said, and that was all he ever said on the subject.

Just before Christmas in 1982, on the day after his 67th birthday, Ken was admitted to a private rest home on Cliff Drive, overlooking the Pacific Ocean in which he used to swim daily. The Cliff View Terrace is an airy, well-run place not far from where we live. My wife Carol and I visited Ken there and were saddened.

The disease had disqualified our friend from taking part in any conventional communication. He sat serenely in his chair, oblivious to the panoramic view, to the singing birds in the courtyard, to—in all likelihood—our identities. A faint acknowledgment, a muffled phrase or two were all he had left to give.

The tragic irony, of course, is that the mind under discussion was one of the finest I have known: far-reaching, profoundly introspective, and possessing the rare wisdom to cut through any situation to the heart of the matter. It was a subtle mind that unearthed bedrock emotions from the innermost recesses of his interlocked characters.

Like Schliemann sifting through the sands of Troy in search of its civilization, Ken—as Ross Macdonald—dug deeply for the essential truths of his own time. That he accompanied this within the constraints of the detective novel form makes his achievement all the more remarkable.

The last dozen or so novels explore contemporary California life with a symbolic force factual studies cannot hope to approximate. His imagery sparkled with clarity and intellectual range. Sometimes it startled. "Audacious metaphors," Eudora Welty remarked of them.

Kenneth Millar ransacked his unhappy childhood to create his art, recreating himself in the process. His favorite book was *The Great Gatsby* and he read the novel annually. Like Fitzgerald's tragic hero, Ken transformed himself in his own *Winter Dreams.* Only *his* dreams fulfilled themselves in his fiction.

Hugh Kenner dubbed Ross Macdonald's books "fables of modern identity." And as with fables the books produced morals, for this was a writer concerned, above all, with good and evil. He showed us that unresolved tensions and family problems left to fester over generations could spawn more homicides than a Mafia gang war, that the capacity for murder lies dormant in anyone stretched to his emotional limits. He invested in detective Lew Archer the same understanding and generosity of spirit that he gave in real life to the many young writers who sought him out.

Six months after entering the rest home severe physical complications caused by Alzheimer's disease dictated Ken's transfer to two hospitals. Less than a month later he died. In accordance with his wishes, Kenneth Millar's body was cremated and his ashes scattered in the Santa Barbara Channel.

He has entered his house justified—forever part of the landscape he loved and wrote about so beautifully. And while his physical body is now part of the California air, the body of his work is permanently established in the mainstream of American literature.

One final glimpse of Ken. It was on one of our last visits to the Cliff View Terrace. On this day Carol, whose powers of empathy much exceed mine, was herself uncharacteristically silent. Where normally she would talk freely to Ken and put her arm over his shoulders, she was on this day as remote in her thoughts as he. The silence grew but I had no wish to fill the air with small talk addressed to a man who did not abide small talk when he was well.

Less out of inspiration than opportunity, I picked up a book from Ken's night table. It was a volume of poetry by the turn-of-the-Century Canadian writer, Robert Service, exactly the kind of book Ken would have read as a boy in Winnipeg or Ontario. I began to read aloud "The Shooting of Dan McGrew" and immediately felt, if not a ground swell of interest, at least a guarded attention. It seemed to me that Ken sat up a bit straighter and I saw him turn an ear toward the sound of my voice.

I read for perhaps ten minutes, the last few of which found me recalling, none too faithfully, some verses from "The Rime of the Ancient Mariner" by Coleridge, on whose work Ken wrote his doctoral dissertation. When I stopped, I felt somewhat self-conscious and on our way out, thinking I may have presumed, said to Ken: "I hope you didn't mind the poetry." No response. Ken's head was bowed. I persisted.

"After all, being read to never hurt anyone, did it."

Whereupon Ken, in that forever-gone, precise, and distantly Canadian inflection looked right at me with remarkably alert eyes of another time and clearly said: "Not that I ever heard of."

And then he smiled his sweet wraparound smile, the unguarded one you do not forget once it has been bestowed upon you. We walked the few steps to the door. By the time I looked back he had returned to his silence.

The last time I saw Ken, his eyes were open but unseeing. We exchanged no words, but he knew where my hand was resting on his bed and he clasped it. His grip was surprisingly strong.

NOTES ON CONTRIBUTORS

THOMAS BERGER has written a dozen highly regarded novels, the most recent being *The Feud*, published in 1983.

MATTHEW J. BRUCCOLI's *Ross Macdonald* was published earlier this year. He has also written biographies of F. Scott Fitzgerald, John O'Hara, and James Gould Cozzens.

JEROME CHARYN's many books include four "law and order" novels set in a New York City police precinct.

DONALD DAVIE, the distinguished British poet and literary critic is currently teaching at Vanderbilt University.

ROBERT EASTON has published notable works of Western fiction and nonfiction. He is working on a second volume of California historical fiction, following *This Promised Land* which appeared in 1982.

WILLIAM GOLDMAN, the renowned screenwriter and novelist, has recently published *Adventures in the Screen Trade*, a savvy account of his Hollywood experience.

HUGH KENNER's profound studies of James Joyce, Ezra Pound, Wyndham Lewis and Samuel Beckett are landmarks of modern literary criticism. He teaches at Johns Hopkins University.

RICHARD LAYMAN's *Shadow Man* (1981) was the first full-length biography of Dashiell Hammett.

MICHAEL Z. LEWIN continues to create Indianapolis-based hardboiled detective novels from his current home in England.

JOHN D. MACDONALD's dozens of books have sold in the millions of copies.

GRAHAM MACKINTOSH designed and printed this book.

DAVID MADDEN, the veteran novelist and literary critic, teaches at Louisiana State University.

MARGARET MILLAR's 25th novel, *The Banshee* was published in 1983. She is working on her 26th.

PAUL NELSON is a contributing editor at Rolling Stone magazine. He is currently editing hours of taped interviews with Ross Macdonald for future publication.

ROBERT B. PARKER's Boston-based detective novels featuring Spenser have earned critical praise and continue to appeal to a wide audience.

OTTO PENZLER is the proprietor of the Mysterious Book Shop, the publisher of the Mysterious Press, and an authority in the field of mystery and detective fiction.

REYNOLDS PRICE, who has produced much-praised works of fiction, poetry and drama, teaches at Duke University.

GEORGE SIMS sells rare books in London and has written several suspense novels set in the world of rare books.

RALPH B. SIPPER has been a seller of rare books in California for 15 years and a book reviewer on both coasts for 25.

GILBERT SORRENTINO has written imaginative works of fiction, poetry and drama. He teaches at Stanford University.

JERRY SPEIR's critical study of the works of Ross Macdonald was published in 1978.

JULIAN SYMONS's brilliant literary career currently spans 45 years.

DIANE WAKOSKI's densely introspective poetry continues to flow. She teaches at Michigan State University.

EUDORA WELTY's fabulously successful memoir of her childhood, *One Writer's Beginnings,* is the latest addition to a distinguished body of work in American letters.

COLLIN WILCOX is the author of a series of police procedural novels featuring Lieutenant Frank Hastings.

NOEL YOUNG is the publisher of Santa Barbara's Capra Press, a jogger of its mountain trails, and man about town nonpareil.